ID0425073

Traditional Chinese Plays

Ssu Lang
Visits
His
Mother

_____

*Ssu Lang
T'an
Mu*

The
Butterfly
Dream

_____

*Hu
Tieh
Meng*

The University of Wisconsin Press 1967
Madison, Milwaukee, and London

Traditional Chinese Plays

*translated, described
and annotated by A. C. Scott*

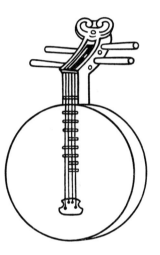

Ssu Lang
Visits
His
Mother

---

*Ssu Lang
T'an
Mu*

The
Butterfly
Dream

---

*Hu
Tieh
Meng*

Published by the University of Wisconsin Press
Madison, Milwaukee, and London
U.S.A.: Box 1379, Madison, Wisconsin 53701
U.K.: 26–28 Hallam Street, London, W. 1
Copyright © 1967 by the Regents of the University of Wisconsin
Printed in the United States of America
by North Central Publishing Co., St. Paul, Minnesota
Library of Congress Catalog Card Number 66–22854

Preface

This book has a twofold purpose: to provide theater students with a key for following the methods used in staging a traditional Chinese play and at the same time to give them a record of two typical pieces which now seem doomed to disappear permanently from the Peking stage. The Chinese theater has been a neglected area of study even with the growing interest in the Asian performing arts so noticeable in the United States today. One reason for this perhaps lies in the scanty opportunities Americans have had for seeing accomplished performances at firsthand. The first and last occasion was the visit of Mei Lan-fang and his troupe to the United States in 1930. No artist of such caliber has come from China since. Political considerations prevented American audiences from seeing the two excellent Peking troupes which visited Europe in 1955 and Canada in 1956; their repertoires, however, tended to be streamlined to a new age rather than representative of pure tradition.

Ironically enough the Chinese stage has been bedeviled by the affection of its own admirers abroad. The deep-rooted tradition of amateur performance and the widespread location of immigrant communities, particularly in the United States, have meant a constant image of undisciplined performance before Western eyes with no really polished art to counterbalance it. That is not to denigrate Chinese amateurs whose devotion is highly commendable; it is simply a question of a sense of values which unfortunately has been denied the Western public. Their general attitude towards Chinese matters in any case has been less than perceptive and too often people have rushed into print with questionable generalizations about

v

Chinese theatrical art based on the hybrid performances of China-town.

It would be a truism to say that real understanding of a Chinese play cannot come from reading a text. Chinese theater provides a total experience for its audience through the manipulation of sound and movement within space, and it is quite unconcerned with logic and psychological analysis in the Western way. Western audiences are conditioned by a long tradition which instinctively assumes that theatrical production is primarily the staging of a literary script, the written word is the essence of the drama. The Asian play in contrast only becomes intelligible through the actor awakening sensory rhythms within the consciousness of the spectator; it is an evanescent process for which a text leaves no tangible record. The greatest Asian dramatists become singularly lacking on the printed English page which cannot hope to recapture the rhythm of music and gesture — the true animating forces of their masterpieces. Literal translations of Sanskrit, Chinese, or Japanese play texts are inadequate not simply because the syntax is different from English but because it is used as a dramatic element to create mood and rhythm that is independent of literary communication.

For the theater student it seems clear that no Asian play can be adequately interpreted unless some kind of translation for performance is attempted or at least a translation which puts the elements of performance before the solely literary version. The translation of *any* Asian play is obviously impossible in an absolute sense but some practical purpose is served if a knowledgeable rendering of the content in relation to the actor's performance and technique can be realized. The results may be far less exciting and even dull as literary effect but they get nearer stage truths, which are what the theater student seeks.

The two versions of Chinese plays given here have been prepared with the conviction of the need for such material after my working with students in the Asian Theatre Program of the University of Wisconsin. These translations should be regarded neither as literary texts nor as complete acting scripts. Rather they are intended as guides, the basis for an understanding which may be more fully elaborated in a three dimensional sense by Chinese specialists.

The first translation, *Ssu Lang Visits His Mother*, is an attempt to give a lucid explanation of what is commonly, if somewhat misleadingly, known as Chinese "opera" and which because of its musical basis and sound values has always been difficult for the Western world to understand. The text is here conceived as a kind of plan by which the reader could follow the continuing stage action were he watching the play and by which the performance of demonstrating actors could be explained to students.

The second translation, *The Butterfly Dream*, is a very different kind of play, and this script was first prepared for use by professional actors at the Institute for Advanced Studies in the Theatre Arts, New York. Provided it is rehearsed under the supervision of a trained Chinese stage artist, this play lends itself very successfully to production in English as the actors at the Institute so admirably demonstrated. This organization has been sponsoring experimental international theater for a decade in an attempt to break down some of the esoteric literary barriers surrounding Asian theater, by enabling professional actors to study live stage practice as a discipline with guest actors and directors. For such a purpose translating a Chinese play serves a legitimate function. One or two verbal cuts or adaptations which were made to suit the timing and staging of the New York performance have been restored here; otherwise this is the play as it was given at the Institute in New York and the Library of Congress in Washington, the first times it had ever been done in English.

Both the plays translated here are popular theater in the truest sense of the term. There are several different versions of each, for the Chinese actor has always been eclectic in his adaptations, but these translations are based on what come nearest to being the standard interpretations. Either of these plays would have received short shrift from the old Chinese scholar but they were not devised for his delectation. Their forms were sprung from a great acting tradition and this endowed them with a perennial freshness for the enthusiastic audiences who crowded the playhouses of Peking and Shanghai year in and year out.

There were at least three versions of *Ssu Lang T'an Mu* in use before the last war; the one on which this translation is based was published in 1937 in Shanghai by the Shanghai hsi-pao she. The script used for *The Butterfly Dream* production in New York in 1961 was based on two different versions of the play. For consistency the translation here has been made to conform as far as possible with the version *Hu Tieh Meng*, published by Shanghai hsi-hsüeh shu chü fa hsing under the general editorship of Ch'en Hsi-hsin, and one of a standard series of playscripts published in Shanghai probably during the late thirties.

A tape has been made of the illustrative excerpts from *Ssu Lang Visits His Mother* printed in the appendix of this book. It is sold for $4.00 by the BUREAU OF AUDIO-VISUAL INSTRUCTION, 1312 W. Johnson Street, Madison, Wisconsin.

Acknowledgments

I am grateful to the Institute for Advanced Studies in the Theatre Arts, New York, for agreeing to the publication of photographs which, though my own, were taken in closed sessions at the Institute and also for their making available for reference the acting script of *The Butterfly Dream* retained in the Institute's archives.

I am indebted to the editor of *Drama Survey* for permission to use the photographs of *The Butterfly Dream*, first published in his journal.

My thanks are also due to Mr. Daniel Yang of the University of Wisconsin for his assistance in making the tape prepared to use with this volume and to Mrs. Florence Meland, secretary to the Department of Asian Studies at the University, for her care and patience in preparing the typescript.

A.C.S.

University of Wisconsin
May, 1966

Contents

Illustrations

Introduction

Introduction

A Chinese playscript contains the barest stage directions, if it contains any at all. The literary content is devised to give a basis for sound pattern and movement achieved through every form of vocal embellishment made possible by the unique tonal characteristics of the Chinese language. The whole thing is simply an outline with which to provide impetus for the live performance of the actor. Language is treated as a physical element whose purpose is not confined to literal communication.

Clearly a great deal must be sacrificed in trying to translate a play of this nature, for bald written description can only hint at the presence of the contrived balance of sound and movement used to create emotional identification with the Chinese audience. The translator is faced with problems which place him between two stools and for whose solution there cannot be more than compromise. If he decides on a purely lyrical interpretation, which has been the general approach for so many Asian plays in the past, he must ignore the relation of the text to movement sequences, the progression of the actor's gestures, the length of tonal intervals, in fact all the attributes which make a Chinese play text a working script and not a piece of literature. The plays translated here were never designed to be read in themselves nor were they written outright as plays. They consist of basic plots which have been abstracted from known literary sources by actors who have used them as a contrivance for technical creation.

The important constructional elements within a traditional Chinese play might be summarized as follows:

a. The use of non-naturalistic styles of acting with emphasis on gestural and mimetic techniques and no differentiation between dance and drama.

b. The non-separation of music as an independent form and its incorporation as an organic part of dramatic expression allied with speech which is emphasized to create sound pattern and movement.

c. The stage conceived as a plastic area in which to achieve spatial precision at the total expense of theatrical illusion.

d. The total integration of symbolism and allusion within production including costume, make-up, and properties.

These elements are characteristic of all Asian theater to a greater or lesser degree; the amount of emphasis may vary according to regional characteristics but the fundamental approach remains constant throughout Eastern dramatic expression.

The Peking Theater

The Peking theater in the form which it is known today was largely a nineteenth-century development, although the dramatic conceptions on which it is based date back centuries in China. Chinese theater has a long history of fusing local styles to create new dramatic idioms which in turn were superseded or merged with other forms according to literary-musical fashions. There still remain scores of different regional dramatic styles in China which, although they stem from a main tree, have their own characteristics arising from the influence of local legend and custom and what is even more significant from the effect of dialect on the musical-narrative form.

Until the reign of the Emperor Tao Kuang, 1821–50, the most widely renowned theater style was the *k'un-ch'ü*, a lyrical form which developed in the Soochow area and first gained the allegiance of theater lovers during the reign of the Emperor Shih Tsung, 1522–66. It was essentially the creation of musicians and literati who wrote for educated society rather than for the ordinary citizen, and its technical characteristics were a romantic, flute-dominated musical style — the counterpart of a refined lyricism in the texts.

In the early nineteenth century there was a decline in its popularity which was hastened when Kiangsu, the home province of this theater style, was captured by the T'ai-p'ing rebels and China became plunged into political chaos. Peking, the capital and cultural center, was cut off from the southern region which had for so long provided its best actors and theatrical entertainments. The Soochow acting troupes were all disbanded, and in the confusion brought about by civil war other provincial styles gained a new following in Peking which was now deprived of the old southern form.

The process had really begun in 1790 when troupes from Anhui were invited to the capital for the eightieth-birthday celebrations of the Emperor. These troupes stayed on, becoming increasingly popular, and the actors sought ways to consolidate their appeal. Over a period of time they began to adapt the technical characteristics of other local styles, particularly that of Hupeh. The present-day Peking style was the eventual result of these fusions and became known in theatrical circles as *p'i-huang*, an abbreviation for the two musical modes which underlie its construction. The Chinese also refer to it as *ching-hsi*, "drama of the capital." The Peking style gained great favor in the reign of the Empress Dowager, 1835–1908, herself an ardent theater fan and the last of a long line of imperial patrons of the stage.

The vocal and musical styles of the Peking form were simple and easy to memorize and not too profound in sentiment or appeal for the man in the street. The plots of the plays were largely adapted from popular historical romances, storyteller's themes, and similar sources. *Ssu Lang Visits His Mother* is a typical case in point. Characters in plays such as these were already familiar within the public's imagination and provided ready dramatic identification. For the most part the playwrights remained anonymous and in a great many cases were themselves actors. They did a professionally knowledgeable job of arranging suitable material for their troupes and were concerned with the stage before all else.

It is enlightening to read the words of an early nineteenth-century connoisseur who in the period of theatrical transition bewailed changing public tastes in these words: ". . . when vulgar low class *erh-huang* and *pang-tzu* tunes are played loud approval is heard beyond the stage but when *k'un-ch'ü* is sung in a teahouse the audience is as scattered as the stars in the morning sky. When scholars gather to drink wine and hear singing-girls, they listen quietly and smile, nodding their heads. How different from the bustle and din of a Peking play."

One of the great names in the history of the Peking theater is that of T'an Hsin-p'ei, 1847–1917, who was born into a Hupeh acting family and died the *doyen* of the theatrical profession. He began his training under his father, then entered a training troupe at the age of eleven. He made his last stage appearance a few weeks before he died. T'an first arrived in Peking during the period of transition and was one of the actors who did a great deal to enrich and develop the Peking style. His name is still a legend in Chinese theatrical circles and his acting methods have greatly influenced succeeding generations. T'an first adapted the play *Ssu Lang Visits His Mother* to the new Peking style, and after 1902 his version became the classic interpretation, and it is the one on which the present translation is based. He made the play uniquely his own and the family tradition was carried on by his grandson T'an Fu-ying, 1905 —, who was a firm favorite in this role with Peking audiences before the war. It is for the generations of Chinese theatergoers of that now distant era that plays like the two recorded here awaken the most nostalgic stage memories.

The Music of the Chinese Theater

Music is inseparable from any discussion of Chinese traditional stage art and in China any discussion of music is inseparable from linguistic considerations. The immediately apparent differences of Chinese music may be sought in such characteristics as its use of an untempered scale or a high-pitched, full-throated vocal technique in singing but these are secondary to the true nature of musical structure. This is first and foremost dependent on the sound variations of the language, technically known as *sheng* or tones.

The Chinese language is monosyllabic and its phonetic elements are therefore limited in range. The deficiency has been overcome by pronouncing each word with different intonations; the tones, according to whether they are level, ascending, or descending in pitch, affect the actual meaning of the word and, what is significant here, create a musical basis within the language itself. This is why in ancient China a high point of musical expression was achieved in poetry in which the rise and fall of the human voice was conditioned by the natural musical character of the language rather than literary emotionalism.

Tonal movement contained within actual speech formed the basis for musical composition which developed out of the relationship of tone lines so that music was first conceived as abstract sound pattern. The composer established his pattern of rhythm based on the juxtaposition of his tone lines and his choice of word meaning was subsidiary to this. As balance, order, and arrangement of tonal pattern were the first ingredients necessary for both musical and poetic composition, tools were devised in the form of rhyme tables which classified words having the same tonal relationships, and such tables continued to be indispensable aids for the literary men, including eventually the playwright. This immediate relationship between language and music with the placing of rising, falling, and poising tone patterns taking precedence over the emotional-intellectual contents of song and poetry profoundly affected the formulation and development of stage technique so that sound pattern allied to music and mime became a vital accessory to dramatic effect.

During the Yuan dynasty (A.D. 1206–1341) the rhythmic elements of song, movement, and speech were developed in new patterns of dramatic usage. A four-act structure was devised for dramatic expression and this became the prototype for stage technique in succeeding centuries. An important element in all this was the perfecting of a song-poem form, *ch'ü*, derived from earlier traditions and dependent on prescribed rhythms, tonal sequences, and lines of unequal length arranged in many variant patterns each of which was identified under a name specifying a rhythmical mode.

THE K'UN-CH'Ü

The Yuan-style drama was succeeded by a lyrical form called the *k'un-ch'ü*. The name can be roughly translated as "K'unshan musical style," *k'un* being a place name and *ch'ü* being a generic term for a song-poem form, as noted above. Naturally, it passed through many stages of development. At the beginning it was primarily a question of modified tastes developed through style differences in music and verse of what were named the northern and southern schools of ch'ü. The k'un-ch'ü crystallized as a dramatic form which was patronized essentially by scholars, literary men, and the Court. It represented a facet of classical art and embodied the spirit of a great cultural past. The exclusive nature of this dramatic form led to its decline and final relegation following the political-social developments in the nineteenth century. It had to give way to theater of a more popular kind. True k'un-ch'ü is almost a lost art today but none the less important, for it was the historical inspiration to the Peking theater that superseded it.

The principal musical accompaniment in the k'un-ch'ü is provided by a seven-holed bamboo flute, *ti-tzu*, and the seven tonalities derived from this instrument provide the different scales. The Chinese diatonic scale is established in seven degrees named *ho, ssu, yi, shang, ch'ih, kung,* and *fan*. A half tone is admitted between yi and shang, and if the scale is carried higher another half tone occurs between the seventh and eighth degrees, i.e., the first degree of the upper octave according to Western rules. The Chinese use the terms *liu* and *wu* to designate ho and ssu in the upper octave. For the notes following, i.e., shang, ch'ih, kung, and fan, the same names are used but a distinguishing mark in the form of the character for *jen* is placed before the printed form of each degree and in the lower octave a mark rather like a comma is placed at the base of each degree as it is represented in print. If we take the Chinese seven-tone notation as given above, we have what in Western notation approximates to C, D, E, F, G, A, B, C, D.

The degrees of a scale are mobile within the compass of the seven tonalities providing the means for seven variations without recourse to accidentals and creating what are called *kung-tiao*, translatable as "modes," which are the basis for musical composition and versification. Within the kung-tiao classification lies yet another, *ch'ü-pai*. This is in fact nothing more than a descriptive label placed at the beginning of a passage of verse and indicating to which style of musical composition and versification it belongs. A ch'ü-pai is usually designated by three Chinese characters, occasionally two or four, whose literal meanings have no significance in themselves but whose combination is immediately associated with a specific musical arrangement, which again in turn is associated with a special dramatic purpose. A group of ch'ü-pai in arranged sequence make what is called a *t'ao*, which in stage terms equals an act. The various musical patterns evolved from the rather complex process described above provided individual mood and movement and within this context the dramatist sought for basic forms to create musical co-ordination for a particular situation in his play.

Recapitulating, the musical style of the k'un-ch'ü theater uses seven tonal variations under each of which occurs the kung-tiao classification and within this the ch'ü-pai, an arrangement of which constitutes a t'ao or scene. The playwright in observing the rigidly observed rules of musical pattern and numerical arrangement sought appropriate mood for his dramatic interpretation within this formula.

Song was fundamental to k'un-ch'ü drama and alternated with the prose declamation, a dialogue between two or more characters frequently being divided by sung parts. Declamation was written in prose with verse forms used for certain contexts, such as preceding a monologue or completing an act. Monody was a basic technique within the content of the play, and the duet and trio were common musical forms. The actor's movements were precisely co-ordinated with the song and dialogue; whatever the words expressed was emphasized, amplified, or supplemented through gesture. The dramatist exploited his resources on an audience who responded to the fusion of poetic imagery with the rhythms of sound and movement rather than to lines spoken by individual characters.

THE CHING-HSI

The pattern of dramatic construction and expression developed through the k'un-ch'ü was carried over into the Peking style which followed it. However, while the Peking repertoire, from which the two plays in this book have been taken, has a technical affinity with the k'un-ch'ü it was devised for very different audiences, and in nothing is this more obvious than in the musical basis. Where the k'un-ch'ü had a great variety of musical modes with hundreds of classifications from which the dramatist could select material for his needs, the Peking theater or *ching-hsi* depends on two principal musical modes, *hsi-p'i* and *erh-huang*, collectively known as *p'i-huang*. The hsi-p'i mode originated in Kansu province and the erh-huang in Hupeh province from where it spread to Anhui province among others. These two musical styles were taken up by various provincial acting troupes, especially those of Anhui, and modified to suit their stage needs. Eventually the actors introduced the p'i-huang style into Peking, where after the end of the reign of Tao Kuang, 1821–74, it superseded the k'un-ch'ü in popular esteem. The two modes of hsi-p'i and erh-huang utilize fixed and limited rhythmic patterns which are defined in terms of *pan* and *yen*. Pan means the accented beat within the bar or measure and yen, the unaccented beat. For example, an actor's song will be printed as being rendered in *hsi-p'i man-pan*. *Man* means slow timing and consists of one pan and three yen, or one accented and three unaccented beats. The range for the composer and dramatist is limited and this limitation makes for considerable repetition. But it is in this repetition that the strength of the musical form lies, for it is easily memorized and easily recognized by the wider audience for whom it was devised. The dramatist by his skillful transposition of identical melodies within different plays can create the necessary musical atmosphere he requires as a starting point, while the actor can enlarge on the musical mood with his movement, speech, and expression. Singing is used on the Peking stage to express the various emotions — anger, surprise, hatred, happiness, or sorrow — and the appropriate mood pattern is conveyed by the use of the appropriate melody within the mode. Although this again provides constant repetition in interpretation it serves a definite function in emotional appeal.

Rhyming patterns are important in verse construction and the Peking theater has a system limited to thirty different Chinese character groups which provide a key. A general rule is that when the rhyme of a first stanza occurs within one of these groups the rest of the passage must follow within the same rhyme group. A common verse form is a division of ten feet, that is to say, ten Chinese characters which the actor breaks down into a rhythmically accentuated pattern of 3–3–4. In monologue and dialogue the first two lines of a stanza are often spoken in monotone with the third line rising in a long drawn-out enunciation and the fourth line retaining an even quality or, alternatively, a brisker enunciation as a presignal for action to follow. The actor's vocal style is achieved by attention to five principal methods of articulation: gutteral, through the teeth, with the palate, with the tongue, or with the lips. The actor knows which method is physically necessary for the dramatic need of the moment. The dialect used by the Peking actor is actually not pure Peking at all but contains elements from the speech of Anhui, Hopei

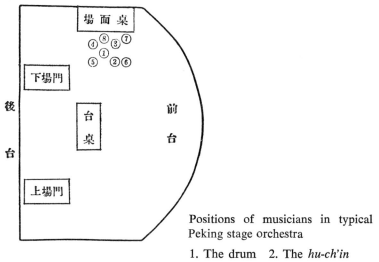

場面桌

④⑧③⑦
①
⑤ ②⑥

下場門

後
台

台
桌

前
台

上場門

Positions of musicians in typical
Peking stage orchestra

1. The drum   2. The *hu-ch'in*
3. The small gong   4. The large gong   5. The *so-na*   6. The *erh-hu*
7. The *san hsien tzu*   8. The *yueh-ch'in*

and Szechuan provinces. The euphony, accentuation, and sonority
of these dialects have been blended in the interests of psychological
effect and dramatic emphasis as well as technical embellishment.

Chinese theater music technique would require a volume in itself
to do it justice and what has been said here merely touches the
fringe of the subject. However, if nothing else, these notes should
serve to emphasize the marriage of music and language which is
characteristic of Chinese dramatic art, while the taped examples
prepared to use with this volume (see Appendix) will amplify the
reader's understanding of a subject for which written descriptions
are quite inadequate.

INSTRUMENTS OF THE CHINESE THEATER ORCHESTRA

There are eight musicians in a typical Peking stage orchestra.
They sit on the stage in the positions shown in the diagram (*see
figure*). At least this used to be the case before 1949. In China today the orchestra is frequently seated in a pit in front of the stage
or concealed in the wings. New instruments have also been introduced and some new musical styles, but we are concerned here
only with the music of the traditional stage as it was. In the orchestra there are four stringed instruments: *hu-ch'in, erh-hu, yueh-*

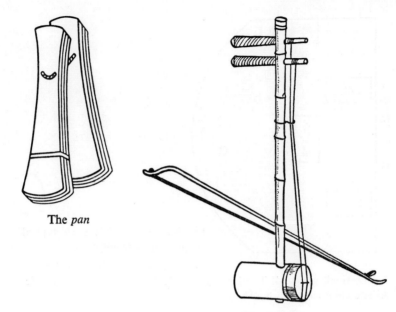

The *pan*

The *hu-ch'in*

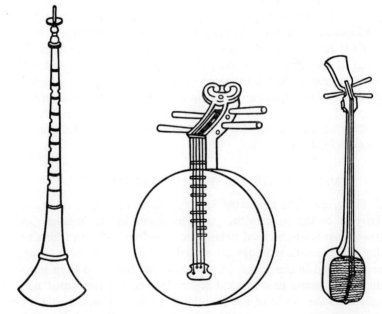

The *so-na*

The *yueh-ch'in*

The *san-hsien*

ch'in, and *san-hsien;* four percussion instruments, *tan-p'i ku* (drum), *ta-lo* and *hsiao-lo* (large and small gong), and *pan* (clappers or time-beaters); and one wind instrument, *so-na.* The leader of the orchestra plays the drum and beats time with the clapper. He sets the time and pacing for stage action and leads the rhythm of song and movement. The drum is made of hardwood and is about ten and a quarter inches in diameter and three inches in depth. The head is convex and covered with stretched hide nailed to the instrument which stands on a wooden tripod. It is beaten with two thin bamboo sticks, or one stick if the musician is also manipulating the clappers with his left hand as is often the case.

The pan, or clappers (*see figure*), are made from hardwood and shaped like a broad spatula a little under eleven inches long. The pan is in two pieces, a thick and a thin section, nine-sixteenths of an inch and three-sixteenths of an inch in thickness, respectively, and about two and a half inches wide. The two pieces are joined together by a knotted double tape. This instrument is held in the raised left hand with the tape over the base of the thumb so that one half of the pan hangs loose. A quick turn of the wrist enables the pieces to be beaten together with a sharp metallic sound ideal for marking out the time and rhythm.

The hu-ch'in (*see figure*) is the main instrument of accompaniment for the singing, and every leading actor has his own hu-ch'in player. The instrument is believed to have been introduced from Mongolia or Central Asia; at any rate it was not originally a Chinese instrument. It has a high shrill pitch and its two silk strings are played with a horsehair bow which is attached to the strings. The body of the instrument is cylindrical and made from hollow bamboo four and a half inches long and two and a half inches in diameter. The face is covered with a thin taut skin and the neck is eighteen inches long and supports two large tuning pegs at the top. The instrument is held in the left hand and supported on the knees of the seated musician. In addition to its primary function of leading and accompanying the singing of the actors, the instrument is used to add musical pattern and color to the performance, particularly in the intricate passages of playing known as *kuo-men* (literally, "through the door"), which serve as preludes to action and song, bridge the gaps between the movements on stage, and in general musically weld the play together. The shrill rippling sound of the hu-ch'in is as characteristic of the Peking drama as the more gentle notes of the flute were of the k'un-ch'ü.

The erh-hu, san-hsien, and yueh-ch'in — all stringed instruments — are used for accompaniment with the hu-ch'in and have a less strident quality than the leading instrument. The san-hsien (*see figure*) is historically interesting as being the prototype of the Japanese samisen and more or less unchanged from the time it was first introduced into Japan several centuries ago. The name of this instrument literally means "three strings," which it has; it is a plucked instrument, a small tortoise shell plectrum being used for this purpose, and it has the throbbing quality of a mandolin in tone. The flattened and oval-shaped sound box, faced on either side with snake-skin, is a little under three inches in depth and measures six and three-quarters by six inches in length and width. The redwood neck is thirty inches long and has three tuning pegs.

The erh-hu belongs to the same family as the hu-ch'in but has a much more mellow tone. It has been played as a solo instrument during the present century and special music has been written for it. In the theater it serves as a secondary instrument to the hu-ch'in.

The yueh-ch'in (*see figure*) derives its name from its circular shape, *yueh* meaning "moon." The sound box is fourteen inches in diameter and about one and three-quarters inches in depth. It has a short wooden neck ten inches long, ending in a carved scroll with four horizontal tuning pegs and four silk strings. This also is a plucked instrument and, although softer in tone, is used in accompaniment with the other string instruments named.

The ta-lo and hsiao-lo, big and small gongs, are made of brass. The larger one is a foot in diameter with a slightly convex surface and hung from a wooden grip held in the hand and beaten with a headed stick. The small gong is similar in construction but between six and seven inches in diameter and beaten with a short wedge-shaped wooden baton; it is always used to announce the entry of the tan actor on stage. Although the gongs are rarely used during singing except to mark the timing, they are used on occasion to control and time movement, to convey certain effects, and to give dramatic emphasis throughout the play. In *Ssu Lang Visits His Mother* the gong is used constantly in this way. There are special sequences and phrases for the gongs, all having their own dramatic and emotional significance when used in a certain way or a specific sequence.

They are used with vigorous effect in fighting scenes, to mark entries and exits, and also to play the *ta san t'ung*, the brassy cacophony of sound which was heard before the old style theater performance opened and which seems deafening to Western ears. The brass serves a very practical function on the Chinese stage and is essential to play action, but it must be remembered that this style of theater music was originally designed for playing on out-of-door stages and that it has retained some of the characteristics of its origins. The *po* or small brass cymbals, similar to their Western counterparts, are sometimes used with the gongs although not in unison with them. They are heard particularly in military plays or ceremonial scenes on the stage.

The only wind instrument in the orchestra is the so-na (*see figure*), a conical redwood pipe with a brass mouthpiece and a sliding brass bell-mouthed opening. It has a small reed bound in the mouthpiece and the total length is about seventeen and a quarter inches with a diameter of about five inches at the opening. This instrument has a piercing note whose quality can be judged from the fact that it is used to express the neighing of a horse in one play. It is used for special stage occasions, for example, to mark a conclusion ending with a wedding or a procession or, alternatively, the beginning of an act.

Role Categories on the Peking Stage

The roles of the Chinese stage represent abstractions of human attributes; the actor does not create individual characters so much as personality types whose specific qualities are taken for granted by the audience. They are largely interested in an actor's ability to play these qualities within the limits of the conventions, and he uses his voice and body as an instrument through which to attain the gamut of expression. There are four main role categories on the Peking stage: *sheng*, the male roles; *tan*, the female roles; *ching*, the painted face roles; and *ch'ou*, the comic roles. Within these main categories there are several subdivisions to define the type variations of the main character convention. Two important divisions in the first role are the *lao-sheng* and the *hsiao-sheng*. The former is always a bearded character and symbolizes man in any period between robust middle age and the decline of life, whereas the latter is never bearded and represents youth. There is a third category *wu-sheng* which denotes warriors and martial characters as well as a lower order such as outlaws or young men of aggressive character who are quick with the sword. The lao-sheng and hsiao-sheng roles are found in both plays translated here, the wu-sheng is not.

The lao-sheng roles require an actor with a good singing voice — the style is well demonstrated in Ssu Lang's first song in the play *Ssu Lang Visits His Mother*. In addition the actor in this role must be a master of subtle gesture and controlled movement as well as quite vigorous acrobatics on occasion. The character portrayed may be a high official, an elder statesman, or even a fisherman, but whatever the role the qualities described above cannot be separated in the master actor. The hsiao-sheng roles portray young scholars, lovers, princes and youthful statesmen, or warriors. A good singing voice is essential and the vocal technique is a difficult one ranging as it does between the more mellow quality of the sheng actor and the high falsetto of the woman characters. Posturing with the fan or long pheasant plumes attached to the headdress is another technical feature of this role which demands a special subtlety and precision. The hsiao-sheng role is one of the most difficult parts to play well; it was a particularly notable role in the old k'un-ch'ü drama, and the real masters of this part are few and far between.

The tan or women's roles, always played by men in the past but by actresses today, demand accomplished singing, dancing, sleeve gestures, graceful deportment, and on occasion the most vigorous acrobatic techniques. Some of the important divisions within the tan role are the *cheng-tan*, the *ch'ing-i*, the *hua-tan*, the *lao-tan* and the *wu-tan*. In the two plays which follow there are examples of cheng-tan, ch'ing-i, and the lao-tan roles in *Ssu Lang Visits His Mother* and a hua-tan role in *The Butterfly Dream*. There is actually no great technical differences between the cheng-tan and the ch'ing-i roles; it is the nature of the character portrayed that is important. Singing is vital in both the roles. The ch'ing-i invariably portrays a woman in unhappy circumstances, and the singing is in consequence characterized by long and plaintive arias while there are many beautiful sequences of sleeve movements and hand gestures typical of this part. In the hua-tan on the other hand singing is less important. The hua-tan is a coquette and the acting depends upon lively facial expression, vivacious movement and gesture, and considerable acrobatic and dance talent, as witness the long dance with the ax at the end of *The Butterfly Dream*. The wu-tan is a fighting acrobatic role and combines all the grace and femininity of the women's roles with the fighting and acrobatic techniques of the warrior roles. The characters portrayed through this role are the amazons of the Chinese stage. The lao-tan is the aged woman role and the best interpreters of the part have always been men even when actresses began to take over. Today, however, it is played only by women, the old style lao-tan actor is no more. The role is marked by a particularly robust vocal technique and its own form of conventionalized movements representative of old age.

Lastly, there are ching, painted face, and ch'ou or comic roles. There are no examples of the former in the two plays presented here but there are four ch'ou roles within the two plays. The ching is a roaring, ranting role noted for the bizarre and complex designs which the actor actually paints upon his face as symbolic make-up. The characters portrayed are warriors, brigands, and the like, their stage technique being characterized by swift and powerful movement, exaggerated gestures, and violent acrobatics. The vocal technique is marked by tremendous volume and pitch, and everything about this role conspires to produce a larger than life effect. The traitors and schemers of the stage are also played through this role although here the make-up is dead white with little embellishment and the gesture and movement, while powerful, often contains more subtle undertones. In its general concept the ching role bears great affinity with the kathakali actors of India.

The ch'ou or comic roles are typical of the genre the world over. Their technique ranges from sheer clowning to brilliant mime and acrobatics, while on occasion the comic actor portrays roles that touch upon the no man's land of the human mind. The comic role is an exceedingly important one on the Chinese stage far more so than is often realized; within recent times the tendency has been to debase and vulgarize; consequently great comic actors have been in a minority. The ch'ou role is distinguished by the fact that the actor is the only one who is able to use colloquial speech which he does to good effect. His distinguishing make-up, the white patch round the nose and eyes, has been the mark of the clown since the beginnings of theater. The comic official is a favorite butt, and in

Ssu Lang Visits His Mother the two *kuo-chiu* make their impact by what they say and how they say it rather than anything else — they are a pair of wisecrackers. The paper boy and the servant boy in *The Butterfly Dream* represent the comic roles in different aspects. The paper boy is an excuse for some extremely skillful mime and dance whereas the servant boy is the perennial fool resigned to the follies of the world and his masters but not without protest to the bitter end.

MAKE-UP OF THE DIFFERENT ROLES

The make-up for the Princess and Ssu Lang's wife in the first play and for T'ien Shih in the second is standard for a majority of women's parts; only the depth of tone is varied according to needs. The face is made up in matte white first and the eyes are surrounded by a deep red which is graded away into a pink merging with the white of the cheeks and the sides of the nose, the bridge of which is left white. The eyebrows and corners of the eyes are penciled to slant upwards and the natural mouth is painted out to enable the lips to be rouged in small decorative curves.

The lao-tan actor has practically no make-up, only the eyes and brows are lightly penciled. The make-up for the hsiao-sheng role is almost similar to the female roles although the contrasts in tints are not so noticeable. The sheng actor uses a very light make-up, very often nothing more than a penciling of brows and eyes and a suggestion of heightened tone on the cheeks but usually there is not even that. The ch'ou or comic actor, with the exception of the paper boy in *The Butterfly Dream* (*see illus.*), decorates his face with a white patch round the eyes and nose with black markings superimposed and differing in pattern according to role. The origin of these markings seems to be lost even among the acting profession itself but they are traditional through long usage and the markings used for one role are never interchanged with another. The most complex make-ups on the Chinese stage, of course, are those of the ching actors, a role not represented in the plays translated here. With these actors, the whole of the face and forehead is painted in bold and colorful patterns, many of them extremely complex in their convolutions and all of them symbolic in some special way.

Costume worn by the Princess in *Ssu Lang Visits His Mother*

Right: Costume worn by Ssu Lang in the first scene of the play

Below: Costume worn by Ssu Lang in the scene where he is prepared for his night ride, after the Princess has stolen the arrow of command (the Shanghai actor, the late Yang Paosen)

Above: Ssu Lang and the Princess. Photograph taken during an actual performance in Hongkong (the famous actor Chang Shun-ch'iu as the Princess)

Left: Costume of a comic actor in *Ssu Lang Visits His Mother*. One of the two *kuo chiu* (the Peking actor Wang Te-k'un)

Headdress of the Princess in *Ssu Lang Visits His Mother*

Right: Costume worn by Chuang Tzu in *The Butterfly Dream*

Below: Chuang Tzu and the Paper Boy in *The Butterfly Dream*

T'ien Shih in mourning, a scene from *The Butterfly Dream* showing the stage set

Opposite page, above: The Servant Boy in *The Butterfly Dream*

Below: T'ien Shih reading the inscription on the fan in *The Butterfly Dream*

Actress being dressed for the part of T'ien Shih in *The Butterfly Dream*

The percussion instruments in a modern Chinese Theater orchestra (students of the drama training school in Peking)

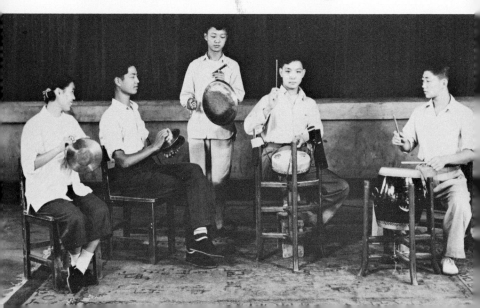

Ssu Lang Visits His Mother

Ssu Lang T'an Mu, *ching-hsi*
A traditional Peking play

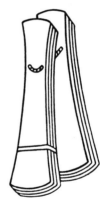

Persons in the Play

SSU LANG (Yang Yen-hui), the fourth son of a Chinese general and a captive in a barbarian state (a sheng role)

T'IEH CHING KUNG CHU (Princess Iron Mirror), Ssu Lang's wife and the daughter of the barbarian Empress Dowager (a tan role)

HSIAO T'AI HOU, the barbarian Empress Dowager and mother of the Princess (a cheng-tan role)

SHE T'AI CHÜN, Ssu Lang's mother (a lao-tan role)

YANG YEN-CHAO, Ssu Lang's brother and the sixth Yang son (a lao-sheng role)

MENG SHIH FU JEN, Ssu Lang's Chinese wife (a ch'ing-i role)

KUO CHIU, court officials and relatives of the Empress Dowager (ch'ou roles)

YANG TSUNG-PAO, son of Yang Yen-chao and nephew of Ssu Lang (a hsiao-sheng role)

PA CHIEH, lady in waiting (a tan role)

CHIU MEI, lady in waiting (a tan role)

MA FU, groom (a tsa or supernumerary role)

YA T'OU, slave girl (a tsa or supernumerary role)

LUNG T'AO, standard bearers, red and white (lung-t'ao roles)

A KO, baby son of Ssu Lang and the Princess (a doll)

There are thirteen scenes in the Chinese original and no curtains. The action takes place in the palace of the barbarian Empress Dowager, the camp of the Chinese Emperor's forces, and the military lines of both sides. The time is the reign of the Emperor T'ai-tsung (A.D. 976–97) during the period of Northern Sung (A.D. 960–1127).

The Story of the Play

This play is based on episodes taken from *Yang Chia Chiang Yen I*, a popular historical novel published in the Ming dynasty during the reign of the Emperor Chia-ching, A.D. 1521–66. The action of the story was set in the Sung dynasty, A.D. 960–1279, during the reign of the Emperor T'ai-tsung, A.D. 967–97. At that time China was threatened by a barbarian invasion, and as a result of a Court intrigue General Yang and his eight sons were sent on a campaign against the invaders during which the Emperor himself was trapped in a certain town. Through the machinations of a treacherous Sung minister a false truce meeting was held at Sha-t'an, where it was hoped the Chinese Emperor would be captured. General Yang scotched the scheme and a bloody battle ensued in which the barbarian king was killed by an arrow of General Yang's eldest son, Yen-p'ing, who was afterwards slain in battle himself together with the second and third sons. The fourth son, Yang Yen-hui, was taken prisoner by the barbarians, but he did not reveal his true identity, merely giving his name as Ssu Lang, "Fourth Son." When he was brought before the barbarian Empress Dowager she was so impressed by the handsome captive that she gave him in marriage to her pretty daughter, the Princess Iron Mirror. The two lived happily enough together for fifteen years and had one child. One day Ssu Lang heard that the Chinese had launched an expedition against the barbarians and that his mother and sixth brother were among the leaders of the great advancing army. It is at this point that the play opens.

Ssu Lang is bitterly grieved at the thought of being so near his own people, including his old mother, and completely unable to communicate with them. He sits down in the barbarian palace to lament his strange fate. His pretty wife, the Princess, suddenly discovers him silently weeping and becomes worried. She wishes to know what ails her husband, and taxes him with his secret sorrow, but at first he denies anything is wrong. Finally, he agrees to let her try to guess what is worrying him; after she makes several wrong attempts he forces her to swear an oath of secrecy and confesses his identity. Despite her astonishment at the revelation, she sympathizes with his fate and announces that she will enable him to visit his mother providing he returns to the palace before daybreak. This Ssu Lang faithfully promises to do.

The Princess carries out her part of the bargain by means of a ruse. The only way possible for Ssu Lang to pass through the barbarian military lines is by taking the arrow of mandate issued by the fierce old Empress Dowager herself. The Princess takes her infant son, on whom the Empress Dowager dotes, to the imperial apartments and here proceeds to make the infant cry by pinching him hard. The fond grandmother immediately wants to know what is the matter and is slyly told the child is unhappy because he cannot play with the mandate arrow. The indulgent old lady hands it over with instructions to return it before next day. In possession of the cherished safe conduct, Ssu Lang bids farewell to his wife and having donned riding habit gallops swiftly through the night to the Chinese lines.

He is captured by a young officer on patrol who is none other than his nephew, the son of his sixth brother before whom he is now taken. Ssu Lang is at once recognized and taken to the inner camp where there is an emotional reunion between the returned exile and his old mother as well as with his first wife who has been living as a widow since his disappearance. Ssu Lang tells them his long story amidst the shedding of many tears, but suddenly he realizes that it is time for him to return in order to keep his promise to his Princess. In spite of their impassioned pleas to stay, he finally mounts his horse once more and bidding a sad farewell rides for the barbarian lines. But it is too late, the Empress Dowager has already discovered the trick and has ordered him arrested immediately on his arrival at the barbarian camp. He is taken before his angry mother-in-law who orders him executed. The Princess pleads for his life. But her mother will not relent. Finally after a violent scene the

Empress can remain angry no longer and smilingly grants a pardon but orders Ssu Lang to a post in the far north out of temptation's way.

Ssu Lang Visits His Mother was first staged in the middle years of the Ch'ing dynasty (A.D. 1616–1911) but only as *pang-tzu* style drama, one of the provincial forms introduced into Peking. In the last year of the reign of the Emperor T'ung-chih (A.D. 1861–74), the play was staged in Peking by the noted actor Chang Erh-k'uei, who followed the pang-tzu version but introduced some variations of his own. It was left to T'an Hsin-p'ei, however, to transform the play into the Peking-style play which remained one of the most popular pieces in the repertoire for decades. Many distinguished actors have performed this play, and it was in the role of Princess Iron Mirror that the famous Mei Lan-fang (1894–1961) made one of his last appearances on the Shanghai stage before the events of 1949, when the traditional theater entered upon a new and politically guided phase in its history. After this the play disappeared from the stage and was seen no more until 1956. According to Marxist critics the play projected "a concept of personal virtue compatible with attachment to alien rulers . . . a harmful distortion of the proper relation between public duty and personal sentiment."

By 1956 when the Peking government issued its now famous manifesto, "Let Flowers of All Kinds Blossom, Diverse Schools of Thought Contend," there had been considerable discussion among stage people concerning the highhanded methods of the Peking censors in banning popular stage material such as *Ssu Lang Visits His Mother.* The result was that the ban was lifted and the play was seen on the stage once more, the first performance being giving during May, 1956, in the Central Park theater, Peking. The role of the Princess Iron Mirror was played by the well-known actor Chang Chun-ch'iu, leader of one of the principal Peking troupes, and the play was seen by an audience of two thousand. There were some minor changes in the play but these were largely physical matters in the staging. The orchestra, for example, was seated in a pit in front of the stage, curtains were used for scene changes, and the stage supernumeraries who played soldiers and attendants had new costumes. The costumes of the principal characters remained the same as before. The text of the play and the methods of staging remained virtually unaltered. In the old days when the Princess handed Ssu Lang their child to hold for a moment, i.e., the doll she carried in accordance with stage tradition, the actors, particularly in Shanghai, usually introduced a bit of comic business in which by means of gesture and facial expression the hapless father hinted that the baby had wet the robe of his noble parent. This rather elementary byplay was omitted in the new Peking version but it was surely no great loss.

Ssu Lang Visits His Mother continued to be staged until 1960, although not nearly so frequently as in the old days, but after that it apparently incurred official disapproval once more. During 1963 a sarcastic attack was made upon the play in the pages of the Peking *Daily* where it was stated that not only did Ssu Lang preach a traitor's philosophy but the family system was degraded by the spineless behavior of everyone when Ssu Lang bade farewell to his relations in order to return to his captivity. In fact, the scene of Ssu Lang's parting from his relatives was always admired in the past by theater lovers because of its technical effects — the group posing and gestures and the blending of various musical forms. The Marxist critic would have none of this, however, and said that those who admired this particular scene were in the state where "stinking fish smelt as fragrant as orchids" and though many comrades would like to have the play rearranged rather than letting it disappear the truth was that *Ssu Lang Visits His Mother* simply did not have a basic ideology which made it worth revising. Whether the play will survive these new attacks remains to be seen.

To the old-time theatergoers this was a play that provided excellent opportunities for displays of technical virtuosity in most of the principal role styles — only the painted-face techniques were absent — thereby providing audiences with full measure of entertainment from their favorite actors. It was a tale from the storybooks, farfetched to the point of being absurd if accepted as factual narrative but good theater by traditional Peking standards in which realism had no part.

Costumes Worn by
the Characters in the Play

SSU LANG (a sheng role)

Ssu Lang first appears wearing a crimson silk robe of voluminous cut, richly embroidered with a dragon pattern and a broad "wave" design as a border to the base of the garment. Technically called a *mang*, the robe has very wide sleeves to which are attached flowing white silk cuffs called "water sleeves." The garment is slit at either side and has a low-cut circular neck opening; a white silk stock is worn above this. The mang is worn when actors are playing members of the imperial family or personages of high official rank. It is derived from the formal official costume of Ming times (A.D. 1368–1644). An actor always wear the "jade girdle," *yü-tai*, with this robe. The girdle is a stiff hoop far exceeding the circumference of the actor's waist and is secured by loops on the robe itself; it is decorated with brilliants and small mirrors. The hat worn with this costume is made of black felt with a high double crown and fins protruding from either side at the rear of the hat. In the case of Ssu Lang it is additionally decorated with silk pompons and surmounted by two sweeping pheasant plumes while two white fox tails are suspended from the rear of the hat to hang down the actor's back. Called *fu-ma t'ao-ch'ih*, this headdress symbolizes the fact that although Ssu Lang is Chinese he is living as a barbarian of high rank in the play. Ssu Lang also wears a full black beard. His high boots are made of black satin with thick white soles turned up in a wedge shape at the front. Called *kuan-hsüeh*, these boots are used in the male roles for all formal official and military occasions on the stage.

The costume described here is changed in the scene where Ssu Lang sets off to make his secret nocturnal trip to the Chinese camp. He then appears on stage wearing a long narrow yellow robe which fastens to the right and has tight sleeves with what are called "horse hoof cuffs," *ma-t'i hsiu*; a wide stiff sash is fastened round the waist. Over this robe is worn a short waist-length black satin jacket with wide cuffless sleeves. This dress represents the formal riding habit of a high-ranking person. In addition the actor wears crimson silk trousers tucked into the high books previously described and carries a tasseled switch, *ma-pien*, which symbolizes a horse. A kind of silk hood with a decoration at the front is worn in conjunction with the riding habit.

When Ssu Lang is captured on his return from the Chinese camp, he is taken before the Empress Dowager still in riding habit, but wearing manacles and minus his headdress. Instead, a long black switch of hair mounted on a short vertical support is fixed to the skull cap which male actors wear as a base for their headdresses. Called a *shuai-fa*, this switch is usually worn when an actor is portraying a prisoner or someone in distress. It can be swung round and round with a vigorous motion of the head to mark emotional climaxes in a play.

T'IEH CHING KUNG CHU (Princess Iron Mirror, a tan role)

When she first appears the Princess wears a robe called *ch'i-p'ao*, a replica of the informal costume worn by high-ranking Manchu ladies until the early years of this century. For stage purposes it is often much gaudier than its prototype, particularly on the Shanghai stage which has always tended to love showy costume. This robe is made of richly embroidered satin and fastens down the right-hand side. It has a high collar, is worn ankle length, and has a slit on either side to make for ease when walking. Almost tubular in cut, the sleeves of the robe widen from the elbow and are cut just above the wrist. With this dress a large silk handkerchief is carried in one hand.

The headdress worn by the Princess is unique; modeled on an actual style used by ladies of the Manchu court, it has been enlarged and adapted for stage use. It is called *liang pa t'ou-erh*. The whole coiffure is crowned by a headpiece shaped rather like the wings of a bat and made of black satin stretched on a wire frame. The shoes worn by the Princess are also peculiar to the Manchu style costume and reproduce an actual style worn in the past. They are called *ch'i-hsüeh* (literally, "Manchu shoes") and made of embroidered silk with a small white wooden stilt about three inches high fixed to the center of each sole. The base of the stilt is rectangular but the sides are concave and narrow away toward the sole. These shoes give a characteristic gait to the actor or actress playing the role of a Manchu lady and in this case the movements of the Princess' hands holding her silk handkerchief emphasize the rhythm of her pace. Although the action of this play is set in the years before A.D. 1000, the costume style of the Princess was not in vogue until the late nineteenth century when it was first used on the Peking stage. In Chinese theater circles, therefore, it was regarded as "modern" stage costume. The use of this costume is one example of the way realism is ignored on the Chinese traditional stage.

The Princess makes one change of costume in the play. When she appears to give the arrow of command to Ssu Lang and in the subsequent scenes, she wears formal dress. Her robe, called *ch'i-mang*, fastens down the front instead of the side and is made of crimson silk richly embroidered with a blue and gold dragon design. There is a broad wave pattern as a border round the base of the robe. The sleeves have wide plain blue satin cuffs and the high collar, which is in this instance removable and not part of the robe, is of the same color. A long single strand of heavy beads is worn round the neck. The headdress is now decorated with a phoenix instead of flowers and has a long crimson silk tassel hanging from the two upper corners and reaching to the actor's shoulder. This headdress symbolizes the need for the Princess to be formally dressed, in accordance with etiquette, in order to appear before the Empress in court.

HSIAO T'AI HOU (the Barbarian Empress Dowager, a cheng-tan role)

The Empress Dowager appears in formal court dress throughout the play. Her costume, ch'i-mang, is similar in style to the formal dress of the Princess except that it is much more richly embroidered and the dragon pattern is one used only for the empress. An undergarment, also embroidered, shows beneath the cuffs of her robe and her wrists are not exposed in the same way as the Princess'. Besides a handkerchief, the Empress carries a small stiff circular fan. Her headdress is slightly different in style from that of the Princess and is covered with hanging pearl pendants which quiver and twinkle as she moves her head. This headdress, *ta feng kua*, is based on the style worn by a Manchu bride, and the whole costume is in fact largely inspired by Manchu bridal dress adapted to give the necessary pageantry to a stage empress. In the old days for the final scene the Empress Dowager used to appear in full regalia, i.e., wearing a woman's version of the mang (the style of robe worn by Ssu Lang in the first scene), the jade girdle, and headdress mentioned above.

SHE T'AI CHÜN (Ssu Lang's Mother, a lao-tan role)

The old women of the stage were always played by actors, and their costume and make-up followed a pattern which is well exampled in the dress of Ssu Lang's mother. She has short grey hair which is almost concealed by a broad yellow bandeau swathed round the head and decorated with a large pearl in the front. The robe, called *nü kuan-i*, is made of olive green silk. It is similar in cut to the mang but is three-quarter length and worn over a skirt. Ssu Lang's mother supports herself on a long stave, *lung-t'ou kuai-chang*, which has an ornately carved dragon's head at the top of the shaft and is always carried by the actors of old women roles.

YANG YEN-CHAO (Ssu Lang's Brother, a lao-sheng role)

Ssu Lang's brother wears a white robe, jade girdle, crimson silk trousers tucked within his high black boots, and the double-crowned hat with fins (*chung sha mao*) but without the accessory decorations worn in the case of Ssu Lang. The robe and boots are basically the same style as those described for Ssu Lang.

YANG TSUNG-PAO (son of Yang Yen-chao, a hsiao-sheng role)

The costume worn by the actor in this role represents that of a young officer on active service. His robe and riding jacket are similar in style and cut to those described for Ssu Lang when he goes on his nocturnal ride except that the robe in this case is decorated with an embroidered flower pattern and his trousers are pink instead of crimson silk. His headdress is like a turban, fitting tightly round the crown, and is decorated with a large plain medallion at the front and surmounted by colored silk pompons. A sword is worn with this costume.

MENG SHIH FU JEN (Ssu Lang's Chinese wife, a ch'ing-i role)

This character wears a hair style called *ta-t'ou*, a basic coiffure for a majority of female roles on the Chinese stage. It is not a wig but is built up with a number of accessories which must be arranged in a certain order. First the face is made up completely and then the eyes are bound back with a narrow tape taken round the brow and fastened tightly. Next a series of coils of hair which have been treated with a fixative, a light vegetable gum, are fixed into place round the brow and cheeks. A semicircular skull cap made of horsehair bound with silk is then tied over the head and this holds the coils firmly in place as well as serving as a foundation for ornaments and decorations which are later pinned in place. A fine gauze net is bound tightly round the skull cap in turban fashion and finally a high chignon made from a long switch of human hair is bound into place at the rear of the coiffure. Brilliants, artificial flowers, and silver ornaments of various kinds are pinned or fastened with clips on top of all this according to the role being played. Long strands of thick silk thread bound to a length of cord tied round the head hang down in a broad band behind the back, reaching to the heels almost. This accessory is fastened on before the skull cap is fitted. This hair style, so complex in arrangement, gives a very characteristic appearance to the female characters in Chinese plays. It takes about an hour to make up in this way and requires a special skill. A cunning arrangement of the coils of hair round the face, for example, can suitably alter a too thin- or a too broad-faced actor or actress according to their needs. Specially trained craftsmen assist Chinese actors and actresses with their hairdos backstage and the ta-t'ou, or *ta-fa* as it is alternatively called, never looks right unless done by these specialists.

The robe worn by Ssu Lang's Chinese wife is called a *shih-shih hsüeh-tzu*. It is three-quarter length and made of black satin. Fastening down the front, it has very long "water sleeves" and a high collar. Narrow white silk piping forms a border round the collar, the opening, and the base of the garment which has a one-foot slit at either side; this piping is contiguous to a one and a half inch strip of blue satin. This robe is worn over a white silk pleated skirt reaching to the feet, the front and back panels of the skirt being outlined with a plain blue satin border. The shoes worn with this costume are flat-soled slippers of black satin ornamented with white piping and with a large white silk tassel on each shoe at the front to show beneath the skirts as the actress moves about the stage. This is the standard costume for ch'ing-i roles. It often includes a broad white silk sash tied round the waist with the loose ends left hanging down at one side. Characters who wear this costume may be married or unmarried but they are invariably of good character, loyal, chaste, and frequently in a condition of distress or hardship. In the case of Ssu Lang's Chinese wife, a second garment called a *lan tuan p'i* is worn over the robe just described. It has no sleeves, fastens down the front, has no collar, is three-quarter length, and is made from blue satin. In this instance it symbolizes an outdoor garment.

PA CHIEH AND CHIU MEI (ladies in waiting, tan roles)

The two ladies in waiting have costumes similar in basic style to Ssu Lang's Chinese wife. Both wear the ta-t'ou coiffure and both wear a *p'i* over a *hsüeh-tzu*, Pa-chieh's costume being red and her companion's green. Pa-chieh's skirt is cream-colored whereas her companion's is white. Both women wear slippers of a kind similar to those described for Ssu Lang's wife.

KUO CHIU (two Court officials, ch'ou roles)

The two officials who are comic characters wear costume which is a stage replica of formal costume worn by officials on duty during the late Ch'ing period, i.e., in the years up to the end of the dynasty in about 1908. Their hats, called *hung ying-mao*, are stiff and circular with an upturned brim; the crown is covered with scarlet silk floss which is attached to a button signifying the wearer's rank and fixed in the center of the crown. A large peacock plume is attached to the hat and protrudes at the rear. The robe, *p'ao-t'ao*, used by the two officials is a long black silk surcoat fastening down the center and having a large embroidered square on the chest and back — this being official rank insignia. The long sleeves have upturned cuffs, the "horse hoof cuffs" described previously, and the robe has a detachable high stiff collar. A long string of beads, also official insignia, is worn round the neck, and the high black satin boots of the old style Chinese official, although with much lower soles than those worn by Ssu Lang, complete this costume.

MA FU (a groom, a supernumerary role)

The groom carries a *ma-pien*, the silk tasseled switch which represents a horse. He wears a red cotton waist-length jacket with wide sleeves, no collar, and fastening down the front. He has wide red cotton trousers which are tucked into black satin flat-soled ankle boots. A white silk sash is bound round his waist. His hat is a similar style to that worn by the two *kuo-chiu*, although it has no peacock feather.

LUNG T'AO (standard bearers, lung-t'ao roles)

The *lung-t'ao* are supernumeraries who represent armies and court troops on the traditional stage. They have no speaking roles except an occasional war cry or cheer and for the most part they stand motionless in specially arranged groups or wheel about the stage in prescribed patterns of movement. They wear their own special costume and often carry long vertical banners on poles.

In this play there are two separate groups, one dressed in red, the other in white. Their robes are long, fasten down the front, have no collars, and are worn with flat-soled ankle boots. They carry swords rather than banners.

Ssu Lang Visits His Mother

Scene 1

Before the entry of Ssu Lang, the orchestra performs the traditional overture on the brass (ta-lo ch'ung-t'ou), used when someone is due to appear; this is followed by hsiao-lo ta-shang, another arrangement for the brass, used to indicate that a person of dignity is in his home or place of office. The actor then appears on the stage, to the left of the audience, and walks with measured pace to the "nine dragons' mouth," [1] *chiu lung k'ou, a point on the stage directly in front of the drum player, i.e., leader of the orchestra. Here he stands and performs a sleeve movement, tou-hsiu, which serves as a decorative signal to the musicians that the actor is about to begin his performance. The movement is carried out with the head slightly lowered and the right hand, palm inwards, is swept downwards from the chest to the right knee and with a turn of the wrist flung backwards, slightly to the right. Following this, the actor does what is known as cheng-kuan, i.e., with the fingers of both hands he lightly touches his temples as though adjusting his headdress. This action is followed with li jan-k'ou in which the actor slowly strokes his beard from top to bottom with his right hand, the thumb being placed beneath the beard.*

After these entry preliminaries which are typical in this kind of

1. The "nine dragons' mouth" is a position taken by the actor on the stage in line with the leader of the orchestra who is seated to the actor's left. It is a focal point when a player makes an entry and is preparing to sing and to which he sometimes returns during the action of the play. The customary Chinese explanation of the origin of this term is that the Emperor Ming Huang-ti (A.D. 712–54), an early patron of the drama, sat on the musicians' platform before which the court dancers paid acknowledgment as the prelude to their performance. Nine dragons were an imperial symbol, hence the name.

33

role, the actor holds the stiff hooplike girdle, yü-tai, worn round his waist, with his left hand as he slowly walks to the center of the stage. Cheng-pu, the normal walking pace during the stage entry described here is carried out with the feet first of all square on the ground and six to seven inches apart. The right foot is then lifted forward fourteen inches and the left foot is brought up to the right heel and at right angles to it. There is a short pause before the movement is repeated with the left foot foremost. In the official robe, mang, which the actor wears in this scene, the steps are square, i.e., from side to side. When he arrives at the center of the stage the actor faces the audience and again performs the sleeve movement described above. The gong is heard from the orchestra and the actor then recites the yin-tzu. This is usually two or four lines half-sung, half-recited, and unaccompanied by music; it is the standard entry procedure for all actors playing important roles.

SSU LANG:
The wu-t'ung tree[2] locked in a golden courtyard,
A long sigh carried away on the breeze.
(The first line is followed by two beats on the small gong and the second line by two light, quick taps on the drum. Then two more beats on the small gong and the actor steps forward, right foot first, turns left, and paces an S-shaped track to the chair which has now been placed at the center of the stage. Reaching it, he turns right, faces the audience, and seats himself. After arranging his robe he then recites, tso ch'ang shih, four lines which briefly indicate the theme of the scene in poetic style.)
Lost in a barbarian state for fifteen years
The wild geese come from other skies
It is difficult to meet my old mother.
How can I not weep?
(After reciting this the actor lifts his sleeve before his eyes, a symbolical gesture for weeping, half rises in his seat only to sink back in despair. He strokes his beard and recites his name for the audience, t'ung ming.)

2. The wu-t'ung tree was the only one on which the sacred phoenix roosted according to Chinese legend. Ssu Lang uses the title in poetic reference to himself.

I am Ssu Lang Yen-hui.
(The actor next raises both hands, the knuckles of one clasped within the palm of the other, and continues his narrative).
My father was the honoured Chin-tao.
My mother is the respected She-shih.
(He holds his girdle with both hands before continuing.)
Because of the encounter at Sha-t'an fifteen years ago, that bloody battle, the Yang family suffered slaughter and those that were not killed fled. I was taken prisoner. I received many favors from the Empress Dowager who did not behead me but on the contrary gave me the Princess for my wife. Yesterday a barbarian soldier reported General Hsiao T'ien-tso was at Nine Dragons Flying Tiger Valley and had fought a battle at T'ien-men. The Sung Emperor himself was there; my mother was in charge of supplies and has also come to the northern barbarians' land. I yearn to visit the Sung camp and meet my mother face to face; how to cross the barrier which divides us? Even if I had wings it would be difficult. When I think of it I am deeply distressed. Ah . . . .[3]
(Ssu Lang gives a long drawn out sigh of anguish. He then weeps, wiping away his tears first with his left sleeve then his right, afterwards lightly touching his left eye and again his right eye. The gongs and cymbals in the orchestra then play a passage called hsiao-lo mao erh-t'ou, and the hu-ch'in strikes up a kuo-men, an introductory passage which precedes an actor's singing or bridges the intervals in-between. In the past, the actor at this point was usually offered tea by the stage attendant. The actor drank from the spout of a small teapot concealing the action from the audience with his raised sleeve. After this pause for refreshment in public, an old custom discontinued in China today, the audience settled back to listen to the famous and very popular song whose words follow. It is sung in hsi-p'i man-pan time.)
Yang Yen-hui sits in the palace
And thinking to himself sighs
While reflecting on events of years ago.
How sad and dispirited.

---

3. The number of ellipses here and in the remainder of the play are an indication of the duration of the sound.

I am like a bird in a cage,
I have wings but cannot stretch them;
I am like a tiger forgotten in the mountain
Alone and suffering.
I am like a wild goose come from the South
Lost from the flight.
I am like a dragon out of water
Besieged on a sandbank.
I think of that year and the meeting at Sha-t'an,
(The actor now stands up and walks to the front of the stage.
The orchestra quickens the tempo for singing as it changes
to erh-liu.)
A bloody battle they fought,
Rivers of blood and the dead piled up in mountains.
A bloody battle,
The Yang family fled and scattered East and West.
A bloody battle,
All the young men fell from their horses.
I was captured and assuming another name escaped disaster.
Dividing my name character Yang, I turned it into Mu I[4]
and married.
Now Hsiao T'ien-tso prepares for battle
Both sides are ready to fight, my mother guides
Troops to the Northern barbarian country.
I wish I could return to the Sung camp to see my mother,
But what am I to do in a barbarian place as distant as
the skies?
I am faint thinking of my old mother
Thinking of my old mother all day my tears do not dry.
(He weeps. The large gong is struck and the actor turns right
to face the entry to the stage, i.e., the audience's left, takes two
steps forward, his hands clasped together, and sings)
My mother
(The large gong is struck. He drops his hands to sing)
How difficult to . . . . . *(weeps. The actor now flings his*
right sleeve out followed by the left and then holds his right
sleeve above his head. He next stamps his right foot once, the

4. The Chinese character for *Yang* is made up of two single characters
Mu and *I*; hence the trick of changing names alluded to by Ssu Lang.

gong is struck once, and he sings the one word) meet *(emphasized by two drum beats)* my old mother.

(The large gong sounds again and the actor's right sleeve is lowered holding it with the left hand as he makes the gesture of wiping his eyes. He then turns left to the front of the stage and with his right sleeve performs tou-hsiu, i.e., the right hand, palm inwards, is swept downwards from the chest to the right knee and with a turn of the wrist flung back slightly towards the right. The actor now begins to sing in san-pan time.) If I wish to meet my mother it can only be in a dream.

(The large gong is struck and turning his back to the audience the actor walks to the center of the stage where a small table has been placed in position with a chair on either side. The actor takes the one at the left. Suddenly the voice of Princess Iron Mirror, Ssu Lang's wife, is heard calling off stage.)

VOICE OF PRINCESS: Slave girl!

VOICE OF SLAVE GIRL: I'm here!

VOICE OF PRINCESS: Let us go now.

VOICE OF SLAVE GIRL: All right.

(The small gong is now struck. This is always a signal for the entry of an actor or actress playing the tan role. The slave girl precedes her mistress and comes on carrying a doll representing the child of Ssu Lang and his wife. The slave girl walks to the side of the stage where she stands at the left of and obliquely to the audience. The Princess next comes out and walks to the front of the stage. Here she touches her temple with her right fingers, mou-p'in, and adjusts her collar with both hands. These seemingly inconsequential but gracefully formalized movements actually serve as signals to the orchestra. The Princess commences to sing in liu-shui-pan time.)

THE PRINCESS:

The peonies are in flower, masses of red blossom.

How glorious the spring with the birds all singing.

I must go *(she points under left arm towards Ssu Lang)* to my husband and banish his everyday cares *(lowering both hands she turns slowly to the left and goes to the center point of the front stage concluding her song with the words)* with play.

(The small gong is beaten and the hu-ch'in strikes up. The Princess bends over as though peeping through a door to see

what her husband is doing. Her left foot is lifted as though passing over a threshold.[5] *Ssu Lang is sitting nodding in despair and wiping the tears from his eyes. The surprised Princess quickly retreats two steps and exclaims.)*

Ya. *(The small gong is struck and still pointing to her husband the Princess sings)* What is to be done? He sits all day his brows knit in sorrow.

(The Princess holds a large silk handkerchief which is changed to either hand according to the needs of her gesturing. Adjusting her collar lightly with both hands she returns center front again and indicates that she is passing through a door by her mime. She walks up to the right side of the table to face Ssu Lang and raises her right hand as high as her headdress in salute as she says)

I have come my husband.

(Ssu Lang stands and standing sideways to face her salutes in the same fashion.)

SSU LANG: You are here Princess please be seated.

PRINCESS: Please be seated also husband.

(They both sit. The Princess has one leg crossed over the other, a posture incidentally which no refined Chinese woman would take. The slave girl goes up and curtseys to Ssu Lang.)

SLAVE GIRL: Respected sir, I hope all is well with you.

SSU LANG: That goes without saying. *(The slave girl goes over to stand behind the Princess. Ssu Lang looks very sad and sighs)* E-e-h. *(The small gong is struck once followed by two pauses and then it is struck again.)*

PRINCESS: Husband it is fifteen years since you came to my country. Throughout this time we have been happy from morning to night. For the last two days I have found you frowning and unsmiling. Is there something on your mind?

5. Time and time again, this action will be noted in the texts of the two plays. It is performed entirely in mime by the actors, there being, of course, neither door nor threshold on the stage. It is one of the important movement patterns used by the traditional actor to divide the stage spatially and in telling fashion. The doors in old Chinese buildings were double and opened or closed from the center where the two halves were secured with a sliding bolt; there was a threshold several inches high over which it was necessary to step in going out or coming in. The actor's mime was accommodated to these facts.

SSU LANG: I have no troubles Princess. You should not worry.

PRINCESS: Look at your tears still not wiped dry.

SSU LANG *(hurriedly wipes his eyes with his sleeve)*: This . . .
(There are two beats on the small gong, a pause and then another beat. Holding his left sleeve Ssu Lang wipes each eye in turn with his middle left finger then flicks his sleeve to the left. The small gong is beaten once. The Princess watches Ssu Lang in detail before speaking.)

PRINCESS: It is too late to dry them now.

SSU LANG: I really have something on my mind. Even the greatest God could not guess it.

PRINCESS: Don't speak of your little problem even if I don't guess the state of affairs of my Empress mother it doesn't matter.

SSU LANG: Would you like to guess Princess?

PRINCESS: I would certainly guess the most important part.

SSU LANG: Today we have nothing to do I invite you to try and guess.

PRINCESS: Leisure is leisure. Let me try. *(Calls)* Slave!

SLAVE GIRL: Yes?

PRINCESS: Turn this chair to face front.

SLAVE GIRL: All right.

(Ssu Lang and the Princess stand and face backstage. The small gong is struck in tao-pan time. The Princess sings in hsi-p'i tao-pan time.)

PRINCESS: Husband and wife sitting in the Imperial Palace . . .
(Small gong. The hu-ch'in strikes up in hsi-p'i man-pan time Ssu Lang turns left towards the audience and the Princess does the same turning right. They now go to two chairs which have been placed at the front of the stage. With his right hand, Ssu Lang indicates a seat for the Princess who returns the gesture by pointing to his chair with her left hand. They both sit. Ssu Lang places his hands on his knees. The Princess, facing the audience, points to him with her right hand under her raised left sleeve. She is still puzzled at her husband's trouble. They both wait until the hu-ch'in has finished playing. The Princess then sings in hsi-p'i tao-pan time.)

PRINCESS:
Husband and wife sitting in the Imperial Palace.

I try to guess my husband's hidden secret.
Is it that my mother the Empress has not treated you well?

SSU LANG *(speaking):* Princess, your first guess . . .

PRINCESS: I've guessed right?

SSU LANG: You've guessed wrong.

PRINCESS *(with a disappointed air):* Why have I guessed wrong?

SSU LANG: You see I was taken prisoner by your people and yet I was not killed thanks to the Empress. On the contrary she gave me you in marriage. With such kindness to me how dare I do anything to her?

PRINCESS: True. My mother is head of the state even if she had ill-treated you would we dare do anything to her? No.

SSU LANG: We would not.

PRINCESS *(placing her forefinger to her brow in thought):* Ah. I know. *(The hu-ch'in plays and she sings in man-pan time)* Is it that you are tired of being married to me?

SSU LANG: Princess your second guess is also wrong.

PRINCESS *(showing surprise):* Why is it also wrong?

SSU LANG: For fifteen years you and I have lived in mutual love and affection as husband and wife. It is meaningless to say that I am tired of you.

PRINCESS: It is true. For a whole fifteen years we have with love and affection lived as husband and wife. At no point have we shown indifference. Is that not so?

SSU LANG: Indeed it is.

PRINCESS: Ah—I know. *(She sings in man-pan time)* Are you not longing to go and enjoy yourself in the Pavilion of Ch'in and the Ch'u Hall . . .? [6]

SSU LANG: The prospect within the Imperial Palace is out of the ordinary. Why should I want to go there? You are more mistaken than ever.

PRINCESS: True. How can those houses be better than the palace. Besides they are no place for you to go. *(Still thinking)* Oh—I know. *(The hu-ch'in plays and she sings in man-pan time.)* Do you not . . . *(She moves her right hand as though fingering the strings of a p'i-p'a.*[7] *Her left hand remains in her lap.)*

---

6. These are euphemistic terms for the sing-song girl quarters.

7. The *p'i-p'a*, a pear-shaped lute, was a popular instrument both in court circles and among the sing-song girls of old China.

. . . wish to take a concubine?

(In literal translation her words are "an extra string for your p'i-p'a," i.e., a concubine. She sings the last words with an angry air. Staring hard at Ssu Lang she then turns round to face in the opposite direction while peevishly placing both hands on the back of her chair. She looks very cross.)

SSU LANG: Ah, Princess, I just now said that you have remained my wife for fifteen years in mutual love and affection. Moreover, we have begotten an heir. Why should I wish to take a concubine? Such words don't hurt you but they wrong me. *(The small gong is struck once. Ssu Lang wipes away his tears with his sleeve. The Princess turns her head to look and smiles.)*

PRINCESS *(speaks):* Just look at you so fond of weeping. *(She turns back in her seat.)*

I've been speaking of nothing important
Yet you still weep.
If it is wrong we'll guess again.
This is not easy.
(She sings in man-pan time.)
It is not this, it is not that,
(Hsiao kuo-men passage on the hu-ch'in.)
Then what is it?

(The Princess points with her right hand outside. Ssu Lang nods his head; the two stand and go to the front stage as if making their exit through a door. The Princess has her left arm behind her back and turns her head to look at Ssu Lang. He looks at her and at the same moment they separate to go right and left; they stop to look and then return to the same position. Leaning on their two chairs they push them forward and slowly, very slowly, gaze at each other. Ssu Lang straightens his chair and goes to the exit where he makes a salutation, ta-pei-kung, in this the hands are clasped in front of the actor who bends his body forward keeping the head and back rigid, the right foot forward with toes upraised and the foot resting on the heel. He then waves the left hand palm outwards, first and middle fingers only outstretched in front of him; next he raises his clenched fists before wiping his eyes with his sleeve once again. The Princess watches him from a distance all this time and repeats each movement after him. She nods her head when

she has finished, indicating she has understood. She takes her baby from the maid whom she dismisses and going front stage she waves to Ssu Lang, speaking) Husband come here. *(They both make the motions of re-entering through a door and stand facing each other but obliquely to the audience. She speaks.)* I can guess what it is at last.

SSU LANG: Then please guess, Princess. *(Small gong is beaten.)*

PRINCESS *(sings man-pan time):*
You are thinking of your own family
(The big gong is struck once.)
And would like to flee to them.
You cannot decide what to do.
(Two beats on the big gong, two pauses, one beat, two pauses, one beat.)

SSU LANG *(stepping back one pace with surprised air):* O-o-h! *(He goes to front stage, does the tou-hsiu, i.e., the head is slightly lowered and the right hand, palm inward, is swept downward from the chest to the right knee and then flung backwards with a turn of the wrist to the right. This is a standard "water sleeve" movement. This movement is followed by a salutation, ta-pei-kung, and pointing with his left hand Ssu Lang begins to sing in liu-shui-pan time.)*
You are very clever, Princess,
You have guessed the inner thoughts of Yang Yen-hui, your husband.
I shall speak the truth, I beg your indulgence.
(The big gong is beaten twice, followed by two pauses, two beats, one pause, one beat. Holding his girdle with his right hand, Ssu Lang turns right with his right leg lifted rigidly towards the same direction.)
Wait a little.
(The big gong sounds a passage, Ssu Lang sings in yao-pan time.)
It is certainly important that I control my tongue, I must tell her the truth gradually.
(The stage hand places the chairs in their original position at either side of the table which is center stage. Ssu Lang and the Princess both stand face to face, make a salutation, and then sit.)

PRINCESS *(speaks):* Husband, I finally guessed your trouble, did I not?

SSU LANG *(speaks):* Although you have guessed my troubled thoughts, Princess, you cannot advise me what to do, it is in vain.

PRINCESS: Speak out. I will help you in any way a plan offers. *(The big gong is struck.)*

SSU LANG: Ah Princess. *(He sings in liu-shui-pan time)*
  I come from the South, you from the North.
  Although they are a thousand miles apart
  We were united in marriage.
  Princess, if you swear before Heaven
  I will willingly tell you the truth.
  (The big gong is struck.)

PRINCESS *(speaks):* What, you want me to swear?

SSU LANG: Yes.

PRINCESS: But I don't know how to swear.

SSU LANG: What, you foreign girls don't know how to swear?

PRINCESS: That's right, we don't know how to do it.

SSU LANG: Then let me teach you.

PRINCESS: All right, you teach me.
  (The two of them stand up and go to front stage.)

SSU LANG *(speaks):*
  I swear beneath almighty heaven,
  A foreign girl below,
  If I disclose even a little of anything my husband tells me
  Then I shall be punished by heaven
  And punished on earth.
  (As Ssu Lang recites this the Princess smiles disbelievingly and turns to speak to her husband.)

PRINCESS *(speaks):* So that's how it's done. Well, I can do that. Listen. *(She speaks towards audience)*
  I swear beneath almighty heaven,
  A foreign girl below,
  If I disclose even a little of anything my husband tells me
  Then I shall be punished by heaven
  And punished on earth.
  (She turns toward Ssu Lang.) Is that right, Prince?

SSU LANG: You'd better add—until the end of life and so make quite sure.

PRINCESS *(speaking normally):* You fool, do you think I really don't know how to swear? Here, hold A Ko and listen to my vow. *(She is holding the baby in the crook of her right arm and with both hands gives it to Ssu Lang who holds it in his left arm. The small gong is beaten. The Princess turns toward the audience and kneels. She sings in liu-shui-pan timing.)*
I, Tieh-ching, kneel and pray to heaven
May the gods passing by hear me.
If I disclose even a little of anything he tells me . . .
(The small gong is beaten once, a pause, one beat, a pause, one beat. The hu-ch'in plays softly.)

SSU LANG *(turns towards the Princess):* Well?

PRINCESS *(turns her palms downward, an act of decision):* I've made up my mind. *(The small gong is struck. She sings in san-pan time.)*
I'll hang myself from the crossbeam with three feet of silk.
My corpse will not be whole . . .[8]
(Big gong is beaten once, two pauses, one beat, three pauses, final succession of beats.)

SSU LANG *(speaks):* That is too violent.
(The big gong in beaten. Ssu Lang supports the Princess who rises to her feet, and dusts her gown with his sleeve; he reverts to his former manner and makes a salutation behind her. Then he performs the tou-hsiu sleeve movement and begins to sing in liu-shui-pan time.)
I begin to feel at ease after seeing the Princess swear her oath.
For the second time I turn toward her and pay my respects.
After this I can visit my mother in the Sung camp.
(The big gong is beaten rapidly. Ssu Lang turns right and makes a salutation with his right hand and at the same time the Princess turns left and makes a salutation with her right hand. The outstretched arm is held with the hand at right angles and palm outwards in this movement. The two then seat themselves center stage and Ssu Lang sings in san-pan.)

8. In the old days it was considered a great misfortune for a dead body to be mutilated in any way, as this meant entering the world of spirits in a deformed condition.

We sit facing each other and I will relate our family chronicles. *(The big gong is beaten.)*

PRINCESS *(speaks):* The oath is sworn now. What have you to say? Tell me quickly.

SSU LANG *(speaks):* Princess, do you really believe my name is Mu I?

PRINCESS: Are you joking? Doesn't everyone know you are Prince Mu I?

SSU LANG: It is not correct.

(The Princess draws a quick breath of surprise and exclaims.)

PRINCESS: Ah, ah! *(The big gong is beaten once, a pause, and a final beat.)* You came to my country fifteen years ago and used false names? *(She stands up facing Ssu Lang.)*

Today you tell me the truth, in which case all is well, but if you don't, then I'll plead to my Empress mother, and brother . . . *(The big gong is beaten, a pause and a final beat.)* . . . she will want your head.

(A passage is played on the big gong. Ssu Lang stands up and lets both arms drop with extended sleeves at the side of his robe. Then he sits down heavily with bowed head and both sleeves covering his knees. The big gong is beaten. At the same time the Princess who has finished speaking immediately turns her head right, with her right hand supporting her child, her body inclined to one side, she gazes down smiling and talking at the same time.)

Oh, you make me suffer. *(The big gong is struck. Ssu Lang sings in hsi-p'i tao-pan time.)*

SSU LANG: Before I utter a word the tears flow . . .

(The big gong is struck. The so-na is blown in the orchestra to imitate a baby wailing. The Princess looks alarmed and immediately stretches out both hands as though drying the baby who has wet himself. Ssu Lang turns his head and speaks.)

Ah, Princess. I am talking to you. Why are you disturbing A Ko in this way?

PRINCESS: Say what you have to say but don't prevent my son from making water.

SSU LANG *(speaking through his tears):* Princess.

(A long beat is struck on the big gong. The Princess with body inclined as she holds out the baby, goes to the right and seats herself.)

PRINCESS: Please speak up.

SSU LANG *(sings in yuan-pan time):*
> Worthy Princess.
> Listen carefully to me.
> *(Hsiao kuo-men passage on the hu-ch'in.)*
> I will relate my family history.
> *(Ta kuo-men passage on the hu-ch'in.)*
> His grace, my father was an illustrious high official.
> My mother whose name was She T'ai-chün bore seven other sons besides myself.
> *(Ta kuo-men passage on the hu-ch'in.)*
> We eight brothers accompanied the Imperial Prince of Sung when he went to fulfill his vows at the Wu T'ai mountain.[9]
> *(Ta kuo-men passage on the hu-ch'in.)*
> Pan Jen-mei defaulted when the Holy Chariot[10] arrived at the northern barbarian lands.
> *(Hsiao kuo-men passage on the hu-ch'in.)*
> Your father had arranged
> *(Hsiao kuo-men passage on the hu-ch'in.)*
> A double dragon banquet.[11]
> *(Ta kuo-men passage on the hu-ch'in.)*
> We eight brothers as official leaders went to the encounter at Sha-t'an.
> My eldest brother who acted for the Sung emperor was slain at the banquet.
> My second brother was decapitated, fated to be mourned at the Yellow Springs.[12]
> My third brother was crushed to death in the stampede of horses.
> Alone among the eight brothers I was taken captive.
> I am Yang . . .

(The Princess stops Ssu Lang by placing her hand over his mouth, warning him to be silent. She points outside with her right hand, suggesting they make sure they are not overheard. The two of them go outside, Ssu Lang towards the stage exit,

---

9. A famous sacred mountain in Shansi Province.
10. A term used for the emperor.
11. A meeting of emperors.
12. Hades.

the Princess towards the stage entry, gazing from their respective vantage points towards the orchestra. The two then return to front stage, re-enter the door, and return to their original positions.)

PRINCESS: Husband, which of the Yang brothers are you?

(The big gong is struck. Ssu Lang smooths his beard with his left hand while his right hand performs fan-hsiu, i.e., the right arm is raised above the shoulder and a circular movement of the wrist flings the "water sleeve" upwards to hang down the back. It is a signal emphasizing the dramatic quality of the singing to follow.)

SSU LANG: Ah . . . ah . . .

(The big gong is struck. Ssu Lang performs tou-hsiu with the right sleeve and then again with the left sleeve. He next salutes the Princess and begins his song.)

Worthy Princess—my wife—ah.

(The big gong is struck. He performs tou-hsiu with his right sleeve and then strokes his beard with both hands and begins to sing in yao-pan time, i.e., in a state of agitation.)

I am the fourth Yang brother.

I split the name Yang into the characters

Mu I, in order to ensure a happy wedding.

(The small gong is struck one, one, one . . . . . one. The Princess looks at Ssu Lang with startled eyes and steps back two paces. The small gong is beaten in a short tattoo. She goes to front stage and turning her back on the audience, begins to sing in liu-shui-pan time.)

PRINCESS:

Hearing his words I am frightened.

My whole body is in a sweat.

Today the truth is out after fifteen years.

He who changed his name is a general of the Yang family.

Thinking of his family, unable to be united with his own flesh and blood.

I step forward to pay my respects . . .

(Small gong is beaten. One . . . one . . . one. The Princess turns her body to the left. Facing inwards she makes a sign of respect with her right arm. At the same time Ssu Lang turns

his body right and returns the salutation. The two then turn
to face outward simultaneously.)

PRINCESS:

Husband.

(The small gong beats a tattoo. She sings in liu-shui-pan time.)
Please listen closely to me.

Excuse my recent disdainful words.

I ask your generous pardon.

I did not know who you were.

(The big gong is struck one . . . . . . one . . . one. Ssu
Lang makes a salutation to the Princess. The big gong is struck.
He sings in k'uai-pan time, i.e., quick time.)

SSU LANG:

We have been a happy couple, dear wife.

Worthy Princess, do not be so modest.

If one day my furrowed brow loses its frown

I shall not forget your favors weighty as mountains.

PRINCESS:

Husband, what are you saying?

Although you and I in North and South

Were separated by a thousand li [13]

We married.

Why do you sit all day with furrowed brow?

If you have a secret, please tell it me.

SSU LANG *(singing):*

These last few days I could not help being troubled.

I have something on my mind but I dare not speak of it.

Hsiao T'ien-tso arranged his troops at T'ien-men

As the two countries joined battle.

My mother was in charge of supplies sent to the land of the
    northern barbarians.

I long to visit the Sung camp to see my mother

But how can I in this foreign land?

PRINCESS *(singing in k'uai-pan, quick time):*

Why let words put you off?

If you wish to visit your mother I shall not hinder you.

---

13. *Li* is the Chinese unit of linear measure, roughly equal to one third
of an English mile.

SSU LANG *(sings in k'uai-pan time):*
Princess, although you will not interfere
It is in vain without the arrow of command.[14]
PRINCESS *(sings in k'uai-pan):*
I fear in my heart that if I give you the arrow
You will go and never return.
SSU LANG *(sings in k'uai-pan):*
Princess, if you give me the arrow
I will return at the fifth watch before dawn breaks.
PRINCESS *(sings in k'uai-pan):*
The Sung camp is far from here.
How can you return in one night?
SSU LANG *(sings in k'uai-pan):*
Princess, with the whip applied to a swift horse
I can return in one night.
PRINCESS *(sings in k'uai-pan):*
A little while ago you asked me to swear a promise.
Before God in Heaven shall you make your declaration.
(The big gong is struck one . . . one . . . one.)
SSU LANG *(steps back two paces startled, speaking):* Oh . . . *(The
big gong is struck once. He returns to his original position and
performs tou-hsiu, then begins to sing in liu-shui-pan time.)*
Ah, Princess,
You ask me to swear a promise.
I kneel to carry out your wish.
*(He lifts the skirt of his robe with his left hand and goes down
on his right knee. Singing)*
If I visit my mother . . . and do not return . . .
*(The big gong is struck one . . . one . . . one. He twists his
left "water sleeve" over his arm.)*
PRINCESS *(speaks):* Well?
SSU LANG *(performs tou-hsiu with his left sleeve, then exclaims):*
Well! *(Tattoo on the large gong. Sings in yao-pan time.)*

14. In the past, the arrow of command was a small triangular pennant
attached and bestowed by the emperor as a sign of vested authority. On the
stage, it is a small property used to symbolize the granting of special authority or high command. It is a small wooden baton with a broad pointed end
tapering away into a short grip at the other extremity.

The yellow sands will cover my face and my corpse will be
  crushed . . .
(The small gong is beaten one . . . one. Ssu Lang stands up.)
PRINCESS *(speaks):* It was gravely said. *(Tattoo on small gong. Sings
in liu-shui-pan.)*
As I see my husband swearing his oath
My heart is freed of worry.
Husband, please leave the palace
And disguise yourself skillfully.
*(The small gong is struck. The Princess goes front stage and on
her way pauses with her left foot straddled as though over the
threshold. At the same time Ssu Lang repeats her movements,
standing with his right leg over the threshold as they stand
facing each other. The Princess sings in yao-pan time.)*
I will steal the arrow of command
And you will be able to get through the pass without trouble.
*(The small gong is struck and the Princess makes her exit,
walking with slow and dignified steps, her right hand held behind her back. Ssu Lang walks behind her part way, making a
salutation, then returns to front stage. The big gong is beaten
one . . . one . . . one. He faces the orchestra and performs
fan-hsiu with his right sleeve. A tattoo is beaten on the large
gong. Ssu Lang turns right and goes front stage where he sings
in k'uai-pan time.)*
SSU LANG:
As I see the Princess going from the Imperial Palace
My heart is released of its worries.
*(The big gong is struck. He turns right and performs tou-hsiu
with his right sleeve in the direction of the orchestra. He sings
in san-pan time.)*
Call the attendant.
*(The big gong is struck. He turns left, lifts his left leg to cross
the threshold and goes front stage where he sings in san-pan
time.)*
Harness the thousand-li-a-day charger.
*(The big gong is struck. Ssu Lang smooths his beard with both
hands.)*
I shall get through the pass.
(He gives a kick with his left foot as his left hand seizes the

*hem of his robe. The movement is repeated on the right side
and with his right hand and foot. He turns and adjusts his robe
again, raises his left leg, and faces the orchestra with a firm
glance. There is a tattoo on the large gong. Ssu Lang lifts his
robe above his ankles with both hands. The big gong is struck
and he strides off the stage.)*

Scene 2

*There is a tattoo on the large gong. The Empress Dowager
is heard singing in hsi-p'i tao-pan time off stage.*

EMPRESS DOWAGER:

Two countries with no peace between them often meet in
battle.

*(There is a long beat on the large gong. Four lung-t'ao, super-
numerary actors, representing soldiers come on. They are
followed by four palace maids. The two kuo-chiu come next
and stand at the entry. Finally the Empress Dowager enters,
she fingers the heavy necklace of beads round her neck while
her right hand firmly grasps a large handkerchief. The Empress Dowager goes to the nine dragons' mouth. There is a
long beat on the large gong. She begins to sing in man-pan
time.)*

Both want to conquer on behalf of their own rulers.

*(There is a ta kuo-men passage on the hu-ch'in. The Empress
Dowager moves to front stage.)*

The old Emperor had arranged a double dragon feast.

(Ta kuo-men passage on the hu-ch'in.)

The Yang family father and sons

(Hsiao kuo-men passage on the hu-ch'in.)

Died in the foreign north.

(Ta kuo-men passage on the hu-ch'in.)

Soldiers, lead the way

(Hsiao kuo-men passage on hu-ch'in. Sings in san-pan time.)

To the Silver Hall, I will study the military reports closely.

*(The large gong is struck. The Empress Dowager turns right,
enters the hall and seats herself behind the table at the rear
of the stage. This represents the audience chamber. The small*

*gong is struck. The Princess enters, makes a salutation with
her left sleeve and going to front stage, sings in yao-pan time.)*
PRINCESS:
Having just now left the Imperial Palace
I enter the Silver Hall to pay respects
To my Empress mother.
(She enters while singing, goes down in a k'ou-t'ou[15] *before
the Empress and then stands to the right of her.)*
EMPRESS DOWAGER *(sings in yao-pan time):*
My child, why are you not
In the Imperial Palace and
Why have you come to the Silver Hall?
(The small gong is beaten in tattoo.)
PRINCESS *(sings in yao-pan):*
Your child was melancholy and weary at heart
In the Imperial Palace so I came here
Especially to pay my respects to you.
(A short tattoo is beaten on the small gong.)
EMPRESS DOWAGER *(sings in yao-pan):*
My child, your words are over modest.
Between mother and daughter it is
Unnecessary for too much ceremony.
You may go back.
PRINCESS *(speaks):* All right.
(There is a tattoo on the small gong. She sings in yao-pan.)
I take leave of my Empress mother.
(She goes to center stage and bows her head in respect. Sings)
I go out of the Silver Hall.
*(The small gong is struck. She turns right and goes to front
stage, lifts her left leg as though going through the door, turns
left two paces and then begins to sing in liu-shui-pan time.)*
Raising my eyes and lifting my head,
(She goes to one side of front stage and inclines her body to-

15. To salute someone by knocking the forehead on the ground. This
ceremony of prostration common in ancient Chinese etiquette was chiefly
performed before: (a) the emperor, when it was called the "Three Kneelings
and Nine Knockings," *san-kuei chiu-k'o*; (b) a government official; (c) relatives met for the first time after the death of either of one's parents; and (d) a
superior as an apology.

*wards the inner corner of the stage. Her right hand is behind
her back at waist level.)*
I go up to see. There is the arrow of command on the table.
But it is in vain if I cannot get it into my hand. I bend my head
in thought and suddenly a plan comes to mind. Hurriedly I
give my pet a pinch.
*(The big gong is struck one . . . one . . . one. The Prin-
cess turns right, goes towards the orchestra and here the so-na
is blown to imitate the wail of a baby.)*
EMPRESS DOWAGER *(speaks):* Call her back.
BOTH KUO-CHIU *(speaking in unison):* Princess, come back.
*(A tattoo is beaten on the small gong. The Empress Dowager
sings in liu-shui-pan time.)*
EMPRESS DOWAGER: Why is the imperial child crying?
(At the same time the Princess calls out.)
PRINCESS: I'm here.
*(The Princess has a smile on her face as though convinced of a
plan. She goes to the front stage, mimes crossing the threshold,
right foot first and stands to the left of the Empress Dowager
waiting until the latter has finished singing.)*
PRINCESS *(speaks):* Ah, Empress Mother. *(The small gong is beaten
one, one. She sings in liu-shui-pan time.)*
The little slave needs spanking, he wants to amuse
Himself by playing with the arrow of command.
He should be beheaded according to moral principles.
*(She sings the last few words in broken time. She goes to cen-
ter stage and flings out her right sleeve in a gesture of apology
and then speaks.)*
PRINCESS: He must be executed.
EMPRESS DOWAGER *(speaks):* Wait a minute.
*(At the same time the two kuo-chiu go up to the Princess on
either side and remonstrate with their hands.)*
BOTH KUO CHIU *(in unison):* You can't execute him.
*(The Princess turns away and smiles to herself. She goes back
to her original position. A tattoo is beaten on the small gong.)*
EMPRESS DOWAGER *(sings in liu-shui-pan time):*
My child, you speak quite wrongly.
If anyone else wants the arrow of command
Certainly he will be executed.

But if the imperial grandson wants to play with it
I authorize you to take it, but you must return it by the fifth
watch before dawn tomorrow.
*(A tattoo is beaten on the small gong. The Princess takes the
arrow of command and goes to the center of the stage where
she makes a salutation by bending one knee as she faces her
mother. She then sings in yao-pan time.)*
PRINCESS: Thank you, Empress mother, for the arrow . . .
*(The small gong is beaten. She turns right, goes towards the
front stage and mimes crossing the threshold, left foot first.
She stands front stage and sings)*
My Empress mother has been taken in by my cunning.
*(The small gong is struck. The Princess has a look of satisfaction
on her face. Holding the arrow behind her back she turns
left and exits. The big gong is struck forcefully. The Empress
Dowager rises and comes from behind the table towards the
front of the stage where she sings in yao-pan time.)*
EMPRESS DOWAGER: Attendants, announce that I have ordered the
company dismissed . . . *(The big gong is struck. The attendants
and palace maids exit. The Empress Dowager goes
to front stage and sings)*
. . . until the arrow of command is returned tomorrow at the
fifth watch before dawn.
*(The big gong is struck with a long and forceful beat. The Empress
Dowager fingers her necklace with her left hand and
very slowly takes two steps forward. She turns left and stands
facing the orchestra. The big gong is struck and with slow
steps the Empress goes off.)*

Scene 3

*Ssu Lang enters wearing riding costume and sword. He goes
to the nine dragons' mouth and stands.*
SSU LANG: Ah. *(There is a tattoo on the big gong. He goes to front
stage and sings in liu-shui-pan time.)*
I take the foreign crown from my head
And the purple silk robe from my body.
With a woolen hat low over my brows

And a three-foot long blue-bladed sword at my side
I step up to the Palace door
And wait, wait, wait, wait, wait
For the Princess to return with the stolen arrow of command.
Then I can hurry to the frontier pass.
*(He turns right and stands facing inwards. The small gong
is beaten and the Princess comes on. She makes a greeting with
her left hand in her right. She carries the arrow of command
which she conceals in her sleeve. She goes to front stage and
sings in yao-pan time.)*

PRINCESS:
I have stolen the arrow of command from the Silver Hall.
Husband, you can fully observe your filial duty.
*(The hu-ch'in stops playing. The Princess goes to front stage.
She mimes entering the door and runs to the left. Ssu Lang
turns left at the same time. He speaks.)*

SSU LANG: You have returned, Princess.

PRINCESS: I have returned.

SSU LANG: Were you able to get the arrow of command?

PRINCESS *(smiles jokingly)*: Aiya. I was so busy talking with my
mother I forgot all about your affairs.

SSU LANG *(placing both hands towards his heart and stepping forward a pace)*: Ai. *(The big gong is struck.)* You failed to remember this matter?

PRINCESS *(speaking)*: You need not worry. Do you see what this is?
*(She takes the arrow of command from her sleeve and offers
it to Ssu Lang who seizes it and places it in the collar of his
robe at the rear.)*

SSU LANG: Princess, be seated and let me prostrate myself before
you. *(The big gong is struck.)*

PRINCESS *(speaks)*: Never mind the ceremony, be back here in one
night.
*(A groom comes on holding two ma-pien, the tasselled switches
representing horses on the Chinese stage, and mimes a horse,[16]
then stands facing front dismounting.)*

16. As with opening a door, riding a horse on the Chinese stage is symbolized by a pattern of movement used by the actor in an entirely abstract way
with nothing but a tasseled switch representing the horse. In effect a dance
is performed. In mounting a horse, for example, the right hand is raised with

SSU LANG *(speaks):* Princess! *(The big gong is struck. He sings in k'uai-pan or quick time.)*
Although we shall separate for one night
We should unite ourselves in ceremony before
Taking leave.
(Speaks.) Bring my horse.
(The big gong is struck forcefully. The groom suspends his own switch by its loop from the third finger of the right hand and grasps Ssu Lang's switch, outstretched in the same hand. Ssu Lang grasps the sash round his waist with his right hand and mimes going through a door where he turns left to face front behind the groom's outstretched right hand. He mimes reining in a horse as he takes the switch from the groom and suspends it from his own third finger, right hand. After giving Ssu Lang his switch, the groom with both hands mimes pulling in the reins, turns his body to the left, and exits while miming spurring on his horse. The big gong is struck. At the same time Ssu Lang raises his left leg as though placing it downwards in the stirrup, his right leg is straddled and his right hand holds the bridle. Then holding the switch in his right hand, his face is turned towards the orchestra. He mimes mounting the horse. The big gong is struck. Holding the switch, he moves to the right as though whipping his horse, makes a right turn, and goes to the exit where he pauses to sing in san-pan time.)

the palm outward and the switch hanging from the wrist by a loop. The left hand is closed as though grasping reins. The third finger of the right hand is inserted in the thong of the switch, which is then grasped and the hand drawn back as the left foot is raised. The actor finally brings himself to a position where he stands with the switch held high above his right shoulder, a signal that he is mounted and ready to start.

In dismounting, the right hand holding the switch is swept upwards and toward the right in a wide arc and then brought horizontally in front of the actor whose left hand touches the extremity of the switch. The switch is flicked downwards from this position to the right by a twist of the wrist as the switch is grasped and the right foot lifted. The switch is then passed to the left hand and the left foot straddled to symbolize dismounting as the switch is again returned to the right hand. There is a complete vocabulary of gesture to represent all the other aspects of riding a horse, and these are woven into the stage action not only as symbolic representation but as points of visual punctuation and emphasis within the rhythms of the actor's perambulations across and around the stage.

Shedding my tears in abundance
I depart through the Yen-men Pass.
(The big gong is struck. He turns his body left, his left hand grasps the bridle, his right hand holds the switch outstretched towards the orchestra. He lifts his left leg and faces the exit squarely. The big gong beats a tattoo. He rides off. The big gong is struck. As Ssu Lang goes through the exit the Princess steps through the door and stands front stage, facing Ssu Lang. As soon as he turns his back she goes towards the exit and stands facing it. The big gong is struck.)

PRINCESS *(raising her right hand she calls out):* Your highness! *(The big gong is struck once.)* My husband. *(The big gong is struck. She sings in k'u t'ou, i.e., while weeping.)*
Ai . . . . *(The big gong is struck lightly.)* Your highness *(The big gong is struck. She wipes away a tear with her handkerchief. Very slowly she turns right and returning to center stage begins to sing in yao-pan time.)*
When I see his highness in the saddle
I lose courage.
(The big gong is struck. The Princess turns right, goes to front stage, turns left and lifts her left leg as though re-entering a room before going back to where she was originally standing after seeing off Ssu Lang. She begins to sing)
Only after his highness has returned
Can this slave be peaceful in heart.
(The big gong is struck. Wiping away a tear with her handkerchief, she turns right and with slow steps goes off.)

Scene 4

The big gong is struck and four lung-t'ao come on and stand at the entry. Two kuo-chiu, playing frontier guards, enter and go front stage where they stand in line. The first sings in broken time.

FIRST KUO CHIU: According to the imperial order of the Empress Dowager—
SECOND KUO CHIU: Swords will be unsheathed and bow strings tightened.

FIRST KUO CHIU: Lead the way to the pass.

(The big gong is struck. The first kuo-chiu moves forward a little and with his left hand motions the lung-t'ao to move on. They press round him in a file, making a figure of eight, and go off. The two kuo-chiu go to stand as though on either side of a gate, the first to the left and the second to the right.)

SECOND KUO CHIU *(begins to sing):*

Everyone going through the gate will be closely examined.

(The two men stand as though on either side of a gateway and at this moment Ssu Lang comes on. The big gong is struck. The groom comes on and goes to front stage, turns to face left and makes a circuit of the stage. Ssu Lang's left hand grasps his sword, his right hand holds the ma-pien. He mimes dismounting and goes to front stage and begins to sing in liu-shui-pan timing.)

SSU LANG: Just now as I left the Imperial Palace in parting from my wife my tears were still wet. I urge my horse towards the gate and there are two men guarding either side.

(The big gong is struck. The groom dismounts and stands at the side of the stage. Ssu Lang suspends his switch from the third finger, turns left and takes two paces towards the two kuo-chiu.)

SSU LANG *(speaking):* Heh. *(The big gong is struck.)* Open the gate.

(The two kuo-chiu go to the front stage and speak in unison.)

BOTH KUO CHIU: Where are you going?

SSU LANG: By the Empress Dowager's orders I must go through the gate on urgent business.

BOTH KUO CHIU *(in unison):* Do you have the arrow of command?

SSU LANG *(speaks):* I have it. *(The big gong is struck. The hu-ch'in plays a kuo-men passage and when it is concluded Ssu Lang begins to sing in liu-shui-pan time.)*

When I hear them say they want to see the arrow of command *(As he sings he turns right to dismount from his horse and gives his switch to the groom.)*

I get down from my horse to take it out.

(He turns towards the two kuo-chiu and shows them the arrow in the palm of his hand.)

Look closely at it, you guardians of the pass.

(The big gong is struck. After showing the arrow, Ssu Lang

replaces it in his collar at the rear right. The first kuo-chiu begins to sing in yao-pan time.)

FIRST KUO CHIU: It is actually the Empress Dowager's imperial arrow of command.

SECOND KUO CHIU *(sings):*

Honourable so and so, please pass through the gate.

(The big gong is struck one . . . one . . . one. Ssu Lang turns towards the two men and speaks.)

SSU LANG: Gentlemen, two countries when hostile are frequently at war.

BOTH KUO CHIU: You are right, there is often fighting.

SSU LANG: Guard the pass and do not be idle.

BOTH KUO CHIU: We have plenty to do.

SSU LANG *(sings in yao-pan):*

No matter how skillfully the southern foreigners disguise themselves.

(Speaks.) Bring me my horse.

(The big gong is struck swiftly and loudly. The groom comes front stage and stands holding the ma-pien. Ssu Lang turns left and goes to take the switch. The groom with his left hand adjusts the bridle and goes off at the rear. The big gong is struck four times. Ssu Lang gets on his horse. The big gong is struck. The two kuo-chiu stand at the right side and Ssu Lang begins to sing at the left side.)

Do not let them pass if they do not have the Empress

Dowager's arrow of command.

(Big gong is struck one . . . one . . . one. Ssu Lang turns right and lifts the ma-pien to the height of his thighs at the right. He makes a salutation towards the two kuan-kung. The big gong is struck quickly and forcefully. Ssu Lang goes off. The two kuo-chiu turn towards the orchestra.)

BOTH KUO CHIU: Ah!

(The big gong is struck. The lung-t'ao return and stand in the entry. The two kuo-chiu stand front stage in line. The first kuo-chiu sings in yao-pan time.)

FIRST KUO CHIU: The person who has just gone through the pass seems familiar.

SECOND KUO CHIU: He who went through the pass resembles his highness Mu I.

FIRST KUO CHIU: Close the gate together.

(The big gong is struck with a quick and forceful beat. The lung-t'ao lead the first kuo-chiu off, the second kuo-chiu goes towards the exit and sings.)

SECOND KUO CHIU: We will report to the Empress Dowager and tell her what has happened.

(The big gong is beaten. He turns left and then right, and with slow steps goes off.)

Scene 5

The big gong is beaten loudly and forcefully. Four lung-t'ao come on and stand at the entry. Yang Tsung-pao comes holding his sword in place with his left hand. In his right he holds a ma-pien or riding switch. He goes to front stage.

YANG TSUNG-PAO: Having received orders from my father, the commander-in-chief, in his tent, I patrol the camp and keep careful watch. *(The big gong is struck. Speaking)* I, Yang Tsung-pao *(The big gong is beaten one, one.)* patrol the camp and keep watch for all the armies.

(The big gong is beaten one . . . one. The lung-t'ao call out in unison.)

LUNG T'AO: Here!

YANG TSUNG-PAO *(speaks):* Listen to my orders given from the saddle.

(The big gong is beaten. He turns right and facing inwards. The big gong is beaten. He sings in hsi-p'i tao-pan time.)

Yang Tsung-pao from the saddle hurriedly gives orders.

(The big gong is struck loudly and forcefully. He turns left to front stage, facing outwards towards the west gate and sings in man-pan or slow time.)

And calls the three armies to listen closely.

(A ta kuo-men passage is played on the hu-ch'in. Yang Tsung-pao turns right and goes to the entry where he sings)

Hsiao T'ien-tso raised

(A hsiao kuo-men passage.)

Without pretext a large army.

(Ta kuo-men passage. Yang Tsung-pao turns left and goes front stage where he sings)
He wanted to plunder our Emperor's
(A hsiao kuo-men passage is played on the hu-ch'in.)
Fine Dragon Hall.
(The first two lung-t'ao go to center stage and stand facing outwards. The other two go to front stage. Yang Tsung-pao turns left and goes to the exit where he sings)
Anyone retreating will be punished.
(A ta kuo-men passage is played on the hu-ch'in. The first two lung-t'ao go to the exit and stand facing sideways. At the same time the second two lung-t'ao go to the entry and stand facing sideways. Yang Tsung-pao turns right and goes to front stage where he sings)
My ears resound with the sudden jangle
(Hsiao kuo-men passage is played on the hu-ch'in.)
Of horse bells.
(The big gong is struck. The lung-t'ao come back to the exit and stand obliquely. Yang Tsung-pao turns left and goes inwards towards the table at the rear, then turns right and goes to the exit where he sings)
Armies spread out ropes to trip the horses.
(The first two lung-t'ao call out, using their left hands to suggest throwing down ropes. They call out a second time as though with their hands drawing swords. The big gong is struck. Ssu Lang enters led by the groom who holds the sword and arrow of command in his left hand. The groom rides to the front stage where he makes a complete circle of the stage. Ssu Lang follows him to front stage where he sings.)

SSU LANG: Just now I was closely examined at the pass. I disguised myself with skill to ride through the dark night. Far away I saw the bright lights of the Sung encampment. The swords, spears and arrows looked like a forest. Screwing up courage, I will ride into the Sung camp and burst in to see my mother. *(The big gong is beaten one . . . one. He faces the table at the rear of the stage as though astride his horse. The ma-pien is pointed to the rear. The big gong is struck one . . . one. Once again he points the ma-pien backwards. The big gong is struck one . . . one . . . one. Again he points the ma-*

*pien to the rear. Three soldiers come on with Yang Tsung-pao
and forcing Ssu Lang and the groom to their knees, bind their
hands behind their backs. Yang Tsung-pao takes the sword
and arrow of command from the groom.)*
YANG TSUNG-PAO *(cries):* Take them back *(as the two captives are led
off).*
(They all exit.)

Scene 6

*There are two taps on the drum in the orchestra and the big
gong is beaten. Off stage Yang Yen-chao sings in hsi-p'i tao-
pan time.*
VOICE OF YANG YEN-CHAO: The declaration of war was sent to the
eastern capital.
*(The big gong is struck. Four lung-t'ao come on and stand at
the entry. Yen-chao (Ssu Lang's sixth brother) comes on. The
big gong is beaten and he goes towards the nine dragons' mouth
where he sings in yuan-pan time.)*
YANG YEN-CHAO: The Sung Emperor
(Hsiao kuo-men passage is played on the hu-ch'in.)
Took personal command.
*(The big gong is struck. Four lung-t'ao and Yang Tsung-pao
enter and go to front stage. Yen-chao sings)*
Hsiao T'ien-tso without just cause arranged a battle.
*(Ta kuo-men passage on the hu-ch'in. He goes to the entry and
sings)*
From the T'ien Po mansion came
(Hsiao kuo-men passage on the hu-ch'in.)
My old mother.
*(Ta kuo-men passage on the hu-ch'in. He goes back to front
stage and sings)*
I ordered Tsung-pao
(Hsiao kuo-men passage on the hu-ch'in.)
To go and make enquiries.
(Ta kuo-men passage. He goes to the exit and sings.)
On his journey
(Hsiao kuo-men passage on the hu-ch'in.)

He met an immortal bearing three Holy Books.
(Hsiao kuo-men passage on hu-ch'in. He goes to front stage and sings.)
Then we knew the foreign state's
(Hsiao kuo-men passage on the hu-ch'in.)
Exact military formations.
(Hsiao kuo-men passage on hu-ch'in. He sings broken time.)
I enter my tent.
(The big gong is struck. He makes a slight turn and seats himself on the left hand chair and sings in yao-pan time.)
When my fifth brother arrives we will attack T'ien-men.
(The big gong is struck quickly and forcefully. Yang Tsungpao comes on carrying the sword and arrow of command and goes to front stage where he sings.)
YANG TSUNG-PAO: With this sword and arrow of command as proof I will report in detail to my father the general.
(The big gong is struck. He goes to front stage, mimes making an entry and stands center stage before Yang Yen-chao. He speaks) I report to you, general. *(He goes and stands at the left side of Yen-chao, who speaks.)*
YANG YEN-CHAO: That will do. The night is late, why are you here?
YANG TSUNG-PAO *(speaks):* Your son has arrested a foreign spy.
YANG YEN-CHAO: What evidence have you?
YANG TSUNG-PAO: First, I have this sword and arrow of command.
YANG YEN-CHAO: Present them.
YANG TSUNG-PAO: Here! *(He gives them with both hands to his father who takes them in both hands and looks at them.)*
YANG YEN-CHAO *(speaks):* Wu aiya! *(The big gong is struck one . . . one. He stands up to speak.)* It is certainly a spy. Order them to beat the drum and prepare a tent.
(The big gong is struck. Holding the sword and arrow in his left hand, flicks "water sleeve" round his cuff. He goes to the entry and stands facing the exit. The big gong is struck. The lung-tao file off on two sides at the same time. Yang Tsungpao goes front stage and raises his right hand.)
YANG TSUNG-PAO: Listen carefully. *(The big gong is struck one . . . one.)* The general has given orders to beat the drum and prepare a tent.
(The big gong is struck and Yang Tsung-pao goes off.)

Scene 7

The big gong is beaten in tattoo. Lung-t'ao carrying short swords come on and stand at the entry. Yang Yen-chao holding the sword and arrow of command follows them on. He goes to front stage and, performing tou-hsiu with the right sleeve, speaks.

YANG YEN-CHAO: Bring in the foreign spy. *(The big gong is struck.)* I will interrogate him in the tent. *(The big gong is struck. He makes a broad turn and seats himself on a chair while still holding the sword and arrow of command.)*
Guard, send the foreign spy in.
(The big gong is struck. In his right hand Yang Yen-chao holds a small wooden baton with which he raps the table. The big gong is beaten in tattoo. Two executioners with swords escort Ssu Lang in. He turns to see who is on each side and exclaims.)

SSU LANG: Ah. *(The big gong is beaten. Ssu Lang steps forward one pace and begins to sing in liu-shui-pan time.)*
There is a roar like a clap of thunder.
(The big gong is beaten one . . . one . . . one. The lung-t'ao shout aloud in chorus.)

LUNG T'AO: Wo!
(Ssu Lang steps back a pace and looks to both sides as he exclaims.)

SSU LANG: Ah! *(The big gong is struck. Ssu Lang steps forward one pace again and sings in liu-shui-pan time.)*
When the Yang family gives orders, ghosts and fairies are terrified.
(The big gong is struck. He sings in san-pan time.)
I will enter the tent.
(The big gong is struck quickly and forcefully. Two lung-t'ao lead Ssu Lang to front stage. They make an entrance and stand on two sides. Ssu Lang goes to the left side. The big gong is struck one . . . one . . . one. Ssu Lang stands with head inclined right, looking at Yen-chao, who with head inclined left stands looking at Ssu Lang. Ssu Lang exclaims in wonder):
Ah! *(The big gong is struck. Ssu Lang begins to sing in liu-*

shui-pan time.) The man sitting above is from the same womb as myself. Still I will not tell him my name. I will answer only when he questions me.

YANG YEN-CHAO *(sings in liu-shui-pan time):*
I, the general, will investigate.
Where is your home, foreigner?
Which is your state? Why have you come to visit this general?

SSU LANG *(sings in k'uai-pan time):*
My family lived at Shan-ho in T'zu-chou.
The house was on Huo T'ang Chai.
My father was the highest Court official.
My mother is the honourable dowager of the She clan.
After the encounter at Sha-t'an, fifteen years ago,
I fell from my horse and was held captive
In the barbarian state. Sixth brother, step down
And recognize your fourth elder brother
Returned to the Sung camp.

YANG YEN-CHAO *(sings in broken time):* When I hear my fourth elder brother has returned to the Sung camp I cannot make out for certain whether it is my own flesh and blood. Unbind him quickly.

(The big gong is beaten quickly and forcefully. Yang Yen-chao stands up, comes from behind the table and takes Ssu Lang's hand from the manacles. At the same time the lung-t'ao file off stage on the sides. Yang Yen-chao sings):
As brothers, let us sit face to face and exchange conversation.

(The two men walk in a figure eight to the table, Ssu Lang to the left, Yen-chao to the right. Yang Tsung-pao enters and goes front stage where he begins to sing in san-pan time.)

YANG TSUNG-PAO: I hear a commotion within the tent and hurriedly return to inquire what is happening.

(The big gong is beaten. Yang Tsung-pao mimes making an entrance and stands center stage facing Yang Yen-chao whom he greets. Speaks) I report to you, general.

YANG YEN-CHAO *(speaks):* That will do, pay your respects to your fourth uncle.

(Yang Tsung-pao turns towards Ssu Lang and greets him.)

YANG TSUNG-PAO *(speaks):* My respects to you, fourth uncle.

SSU LANG *(speaks):* Please, no ceremony. Sixth brother, who is this?

YANG YEN-CHAO *(speaks):* Your nephew, Tsung-pao.

SSU LANG *(speaks):* How old is he?

YANG YEN-CHAO *(speaks):* Fourteen years of age.

SSU LANG *(stands up and speaks in a voice filled with emotion):* It is a joy to see the new generation of the Yang family. I thank the gods.

(At the same time Yang Yen-chao goes to the front stage and makes a salutation before speaking.)

YANG YEN-CHAO: We ought to thank the gods. Please be seated, fourth brother. For fifteen years you were lost in a foreign land. How did you escape from the tiger's mouth?

(The big gong is struck five times. Ssu Lang and Yen-chao return to their seats.)

SSU LANG: Ah. *(The big gong is struck once. Ssu Lang's hands are placed against his heart, right over left. Speaks):* It is difficult to say a word.

(He begins to sing in hsi-p'i k'uai-yuan-pan time.)

We brothers were separated

(Hsiao kuo-men passage on the hu-ch'in.)

For fifteen years.

(Ta kuo-men passage on the hu-ch'in.)

Even a hardhearted man would have shed tears.

When I heard our old mother was coming to the
North I disguised myself and came over to the
Sung camp in the dark night to visit her.

(A hsiao kuo-men passage is played on the hu-ch'in and Yang Yen-chao begins to sing.)

YANG YEN-CHAO:

Fourth brother, since you were lost in the foreign camp,
Our mother wept for you
Your wife worried about you until she was worn out.

(A ta kuo-men passage is played on the hu-ch'in.)

Tsung-pao, my son, come forward.

(A hsiao kuo-men passage is played. Tsung-pao stands and his father hands him an order flag over the table. This is a banner used in the Chinese theater to symbolize military sanction. The flag is white with a red border and has the character "ling" embroidered in black. Yen-chao sings)

Issue orders to the troops not to discuss this in public. Any violation will be dealt with through military discipline.

(Tsung-pao takes the flag and sings in yao-pan time.)

YANG TSUNG-PAO: Receiving orders from my father, the general, in his tent, I will order the troops not to talk aloud. *(The big gong is beaten and he goes off. Ssu Lang sings yao-pan time.)*

SSU LANG: Worthy brother, where is our old mother?

YANG YEN-CHAO *(sings):*

At present in a rear tent studying the line of battle.

SSU LANG *(singing):*

Worthy brother, may I trouble you to lead the way.
When mother and son meet there will be painful
Wounds in the heart.

(The big gong is struck. He turns left and, with hands behind his back, follows Yang Yen-chao off.)

Scene 8

The big gong is struck quickly and forcefully. Eighth elder sister and ninth younger sister, who act as ladies-in-waiting, come on and stand at the entry. They are followed by She T'ai-chün, the old mother. She leans on a long wooden staff topped by a carved dragon's head and is dressed in the fashion described previously. She goes to the nine dragons' mouth and, following three sharp beats on the drum in the orchestra, begins to sing in san-pan time.

T'AI CHÜN: The Sung Emperor himself is in command at the Northern Pass. Two hostile countries move their troops. My sixth son was appointed a general in the Golden Hall. He asked me to come North from the T'ien Po mansion. Lead the way, eighth and ninth sisters.

(The big gong is struck. T'ai-chün makes her way to the left chair, where she seats herself; the two sisters separate and stand one on either side. Sings in san-pan time.)

How brightly the wick in the lamp sparkles.[17]
What does it portend?

17. This refers to the Chinese saying, *Teng-hua pao, hsi lai tao,* "When the lamp wick crackles joy is at hand."

(The big gong is struck quickly and forcibly. Yang Yen-chao pulls Ssu Lang on stage and they go to the front, Yen-chao at the left, Ssu Lang at the right.)

YANG YEN-CHAO *(sings):* Fourth brother, please wait here at the rear of the camp.

SSU LANG *(sings):* Worthy brother, please inform our old mother. *(The big gong is struck. Ssu Lang shows signs of agitation. He rubs his hands together in a circular motion. Yen-chao goes front stage and mimes an entry, going towards T'ai-chün at the left hand side. When he is before her he speaks in a respectful manner.)*

YANG YEN-CHAO *(speaks):* I report to you, mother.

T'AI CHÜN *(speaks):* No ceremony. The night is late. What brings you here?

YANG YEN-CHAO *(speaks):* Our fourth elder brother has returned. *(The old lady gives a start of surprise.)*

T'AI CHÜN: Which fourth elder brother?

YANG YEN-CHAO: Yen-hui, our fourth elder brother who has been held in a barbarian land for fifteen years has returned.

T'AI CHÜN: Wo! *(The big gong is beaten in tattoo.)* My son Yen-hui has returned? Where is he now?

YANG YEN-CHAO: He is outside the tent at this moment.

T'AI CHÜN: Quick, quick, call him to come in!

YANG YEN-CHAO: I will obey your order. *(He goes front stage and mimes making an exit. He then speaks to Ssu Lang.)* Fourth brother, our mother summons you.

SSU LANG: Wo! Yes, yes, yes.

(The big gong is beaten one . . . one . . . one. When he has finished speaking Yen-chao goes back through the imagined entry to his original position. Ssu Lang goes to front stage and makes his entry, he goes to the left as T'ai-chün stands up. The big gong is struck. Mother and son look at each other. Both the sisters arrange themselves at the right facing each other. Ssu Lang goes to the left and faces Yang Yen-chao. Mother and son speak in unison.)

T'AI CHÜN: Is it Yen-hui, my son?

SSU LANG: Is this my mother?

YANG YEN-CHAO AND SISTERS *(speak in unison):* Truly.

T'ai-chün raises her right hand. Ssu Lang takes off his head-dress, releases the shuai-fa, the long plume of hair fixed to his

*crown, and swings it round in one powerful sweep. The big gong
is beaten in tattoo. Ssu Lang kneels before his mother. The big
gong is struck and T'ai-chün begins to sing in hsi-p'i fan-tao-
pan timing, a melancholy, even tragic mode.)*

T'AI CHÜN: On meeting, my tears flow abundantly.

*(The big gong is struck. Mother and son cry out after speaking
alternatively.)*

T'AI CHÜN: Yen-hui!

SSU LANG: Mother!

T'AI CHÜN: My son!

SSU LANG: My old mother!

TOGETHER: Ah!

T'AI CHÜN: Ah, my son!

SSU LANG: Ah, my mother!

*(The big gong is struck. Ssu Lang stands up. T'ai-chün sings
in liu-shui-pan time.)*

T'AI CHÜN: On meeting my son tears run down my cheeks.

One by one, my tear drops fell after the Sha-t'an encounter.
At that slaughter the Yang family suffered the worst fate. Your
first elder brother was slain by a spear; your second elder
brother was decapitated by a short sword. Your third elder
brother was trampled to death by stampeding horses. Your
fifth brother became a monk and had his hair shaven on the
Wu-t'ai mountain. Your sixth younger brother was the general who defended the Three Passes. Your seventh younger
brother suffered a miserable fate and was hung from a banana
tree to be shot by arrows and died without burial. Your eighth
brother was lost in a barbarian state. Only eighth elder sister
and ninth younger sister remain to wait on me. *(The big gong
is struck.)*

Mother and sons were not able to be together.

(The big gong is sounded.)

And now I see my son.

*(She flicks her right sleeve round and stamps her right foot.
Mother and son weep together. Then wiping her eyes T'ai-chün
sings in yao-pan time)*

What wind has blown you here to visit this camp?

*(The big gong is beaten. Ssu Lang leads his mother with both
hands and assists her to be seated. Standing at her left side
with his right hand on her shoulder he sings in san-pan time)*

SSU LANG: My old mother, please sit above so that your son may prostrate himself before you.

(He goes front stage. Both hands touch his head, he arranges his beard, his right hand grasps his sash to touch his left shoulder, his left hand grasps the sash to touch his right shoulder. He changes hands again and flicks his satin boots; his shuai-fa, or plume of hair, hangs to the right. He next turns right, goes toward his mother and kneels, making three k'ou-t'ou or obeisances. He swings the shuai-fa round three times, each time touching the ground with his forehead, the shuai-fa to the right side. He then stands up, turns left, and goes to front stage. He makes a right turn and goes to stand two paces in front of his mother to whom he makes a salutation, ch'ing-an, which is performed by bending one knee to the person addressed. He then stands to the left of his mother. The big gong is beaten. He exclaims)

Ah, mother . . . *(He begins to sing in erh-liu-pan.)*

My old mother, a thousand prostrations, ten thousand, will not compensate for your son's sins. At the Sha-t'an encounter my horse stumbled in the battle line and I fell in the dust. The Empress Dowager treated your son with kindness deep as the ocean. I was given the Iron Mirror Princess in marriage. All the years in a foreign land the thought of my old mother was always in my heart. I was reluctant to wear a foreign crown and robe. Every year the flowers blossomed they did not blossom in your son's heart. When I heard my old mother had reached the North I disguised myself to visit the Sung camp and see my mother. My rueful countenance disappears. My old mother, I wish you happiness and a long life free from troubles.

T'AI CHÜN: Hearing his words I am glad in heart. He is married to the Iron Mirror Princess. Do you as husband and wife love each other deeply? The Princess, is she virtuous and talented or not? *(The big gong is beaten. Ssu Lang sings in liu-shui-pan time.)*

SSU LANG: The Iron Mirror Princess is really lovable and we have a baby son. She would come over and pay respects to you in person but because our two countries are at war it is impossible for her to come.

(The big gong is struck.)

T'AI CHÜN *(standing up, sings):* I look towards that foreign state and extend my deep thanks to my daughter-in-law of lofty virtue who cannot come.

(She seats herself again. The big gong is struck. Ssu Lang turns left and faces Yang Yen-chao and sings in san-pan time.)

SSU LANG: Sixth brother, let me kneel before you. *(The big gong is struck quickly and forcefully. Ssu Lang kneels and salutes his brother.)* Worthy brother, you will have the tablet of filial piety hung up for you.

(The big gong is beaten in tattoo. Yang Yen-chao sings in yao-pan time.)

YANG YEN-CHAO:
What are you saying?
Why should I have a tablet of filial piety?
It is my duty to wait on our old mother
Morning and night.
(The big gong is struck. Ssu Lang turns right towards eighth elder sister and ninth younger sister and sings in san-pan time.)

SSU LANG: Worthy sisters, let me salute you. *(The big gong is struck quickly and forcefully. Ssu Lang makes a salutation towards the two sisters and sings)* Your foolish elder brother has no talents.

(The big gong is struck. The two sisters sing)

EIGHTH AND NINTH SISTERS: Fourth elder brother, please don't stand on ceremony. It was our duty to wait on our old mother.

(The big gong is beaten in tattoo. The old mother cries out.)

T'AI CHÜN: Aiya! Ah, son! *(The big gong is struck one . . . one . . . one. She begins to sing in san-pan time.)*

Your wife wept her eyes out for you, for fifteen years she has not dressed her coiffure.[18]

(The big gong is beaten in tattoo. Ssu Lang sweeps his shuai-fa round with a single twist of the head. With his right hand he pushes it to the rear and with his left hand against his heart he stamps his foot once and exclaims.)

SSU LANG: Aiya! *(The big gong is beaten rapidly. Ssu Lang begins to sing in san-pan time.)*

18. A reference to the fact that when a husband died or disappeared the wife had to observe strict mourning rites which required her to forego personal adornment and decorative clothing.

When I hear these words the tears flow down my cheeks.
(The big gong is struck once.)
Even the most hardhearted man would grieve.
(The big gong is struck once.)
Worthy sisters, where is your fourth sister-in-law now?
(The big gong is beaten in tattoo.)
EIGHTH AND NINTH SISTERS *(sing in unison):* She has remained in
the rear tent and has not yet come out.
(The big gong is beaten in tattoo. Ssu Lang sings in san-pan time.)
SSU LANG: Worthy sisters, may I trouble you to lead the way.
(The big gong is beaten. Ssu Lang goes to front stage, his right hand grasps his sash as he raises his left leg to make an entrance. The big gong is struck. The old lady speaks tearfully.)
T'AI CHÜN: Ai. Ah, son!
SSU LANG *(in tearful response):* Mother. *(The big gong is beaten in tattoo. Ssu Lang lets his sash fall, turns left, and begins to sing)*
I will go to the rear tent to meet your daughter-in-law, your
son's wife, that lady in distress. Aiya! Mother.
(The big gong is struck. Ssu Lang goes to the center stage and salutes his mother by inclining one knee. He then turns left and goes to the front stage, his right hand holding his sash as he makes an exit, left foot first. He sings)
I am going now, I will return shortly.
(The big gong is struck. The old mother sings.)
T'AI CHÜN: Sixth son goes to arrange the tent for a banquet.
(The big gong is struck. Yang Yen-chao goes off. The old mother goes to front stage.)
When husband and wife meet face to face, their hearts will be
overflowing.
(The big gong is struck and the old lady turns left and goes off.)

Scene 9

The small gong is beaten. Ssu Lang's first wife comes on and goes over to the nine dragons' mouth where she begins to sing. She is wearing the ch'ing-i style dress.

MENG SHIH FU JEN:
    I ponder—
    (Hsiao kuo-men passage on the hu-ch'in.)
    My sad fate.
    (Ta kuo-men passage on the hu-ch'in. She goes to front stage and continues to sing.)
    A single hibiscus blossom opening by itself
    (Ta kuo-men passage is played on the hu-ch'in.)
    A husband lost in a foreign state—
    (Hsiao kuo-men passage is played on the hu-ch'in.)
    For fifteen years.
    I do not know if the day of his return will ever come.
    (Hsiao kuo-men passage is played on the hu-ch'in. She seats herself on the left hand chair. The big gong is struck. Eighth older sister and ninth younger sister come on leading Ssu Lang. The two women go to the left, Ssu Lang to the right. Eighth sister sings in san-pan time.)
EIGHTH SISTER: Fourth brother, wait in the rear of the camp.
NINTH SISTER *(sings):* We will tell fourth sister-in-law.
    (The big gong is struck. The two sisters go front stage and make an entry together. They go up to Ssu Lang's wife from two sides. They speak in unison.)
EIGHTH AND NINTH SISTERS: Our respects to you, fourth sister-in-law.
MENG SHIH FU JEN *(speaks):* Don't stand on ceremony. The night is late. What brings you here, worthy sisters?
EIGHTH AND NINTH SISTERS: Congratulations, fourth sister-in-law. Congratulations. *(The small gong is struck one . . . one.)*
MENG SHIH FU JEN *(surprised):* What have you come to congratulate me about?
EIGHTH AND NINTH SISTERS *(together):* Fourth brother has returned
MENG SHIH FU JEN: Which fourth brother?
EIGHTH AND NINTH SISTERS: The fourth brother who has been lost in a barbarian state for fifteen years.
MENG SHIH FU JEN: Where is he now?
EIGHTH AND NINTH SISTERS: He is now outside the tent.
MENG SHIH FU JEN *(rising agitatedly):* Quickly, quickly, ask him in!
    (The big gong is struck one . . . one . . . one. The wife

turns and takes off her p'ei, a robe representing a formal garment for receiving anyone. In this case as her husband is arriving it is a sign of an intimate relationship to take it off. The two sisters go to front stage and make an exit together. They speak to Ssu Lang.)

EIGHTH AND NINTH SISTERS: Fourth brother, fourth sister-in-law invites you to come inside.

(The two sisters re-enter and go back to their original position. Ssu Lang follows them and stands facing his first wife. The big gong is struck one . . . one. Husband and wife turn their heads simultaneously towards the two sisters.)

MENG SHIH FU JEN: This is your fourth brother?

SSU LANG: This is your fourth sister-in-law?

EIGHTH AND NINTH SISTERS: Indeed it is!

(The big gong is struck. Ssu Lang and his wife cry out simultaneously.)

SSU LANG: My wife.

MENG SHIH FU JEN: My husband.

SSU LANG: Madame Meng!

MENG SHIH FU JEN: Respected husband!

SSU LANG: Ai! Ah, wife!

MENG SHIH FU JEN: Ah, husband!

(The big gong is struck. The two of them kneel, Ssu Lang supported on his right knee. The big gong is struck. The wife begins to sing)

MENG SHIH FU JEN *(sings in tao-pan time):* When I see my husband again my tears flow down my cheeks.

(The big gong is struck. Husband and wife cry out alternately once more.)

SSU LANG: My wife!

MENG SHIH FU JEN: Respected husband!

TOGETHER: Aiya! My . . .

(The big gong is struck. Ssu Lang turns his head left, his wife turns her head right. They both look at the two sisters who modestly hide their faces with their sleeves. The big gong is struck and the two sisters go off. Ssu Lang and his wife smile at each other and cry out)

Ah, husband!

Ah, wife!

(The big gong is struck and Ssu Lang's wife sings in liu-shui-pan timing.)

MENG SHIH FU JEN:

Slowly the teardrops fall.

Since you went to the encounter at Sha-t'an I thought you were lost.

(She changes to san-pan time. The big gong is beaten. Ssu Lang sings in liu-shui-pan time.)

SSU LANG:

After the Sha-t'an defeat

I concealed my true name to avoid trouble

The Empress Dowager showed me great favor.

I was married to the Iron Mirror Princess.

When I heard my old mother was coming to the North

I disguised myself and returned to this camp,

First to see my mother and inquire after her well-being,

Secondly, worthy wife, to relieve the feelings in

Your heart.

(His wife has turned away from him during his confession, she now turns towards him again and sings in liu-shui-pan time.)

MENG SHIH FU JEN: When I hear your words I am unhappy. You married the Iron Mirror Princess. Because of you I did not wear flowers in my hair. Because of you I did not wear embroidered shoes. I did not eat, I could not drink tea. For fifteen years I have not sat down at my dressing table to do my coiffure.

(The big gong is struck one . . . one . . . one. Ssu Lang calls out.)

SSU LANG: Ah, my wife. *(He begins to sing in liu-shui-pan time.)* Worthy wife, refrain from blaming me. Listen to what I have to say, put aside your bitterness. If the Princess had not stolen the arrow of command so quickly I would not have been able to return at all. We are united.

(The big gong is struck one . . . one . . . one.)

Compelled to weep,

(The big gong is struck.)

My whole being is afflicted.

(With his left hand Ssu Lang flings his beard to one side and stamps his left foot. With his right hand he then pushes his

beard to the right side and stamps his right foot. He raises his right hand and gestures boldly with the second and middle finger pointing.)

Ah, my wife . . . *(The big gong is beaten in tattoo. The orchestra drum beats out four strokes. Ssu Lang turns towards the orchestra and counts out each stroke with the fingers of his right hand, beginning with the little finger. He calls out)* Aiya! *(The big gong is struck and he begins to sing in san-pan time.)*
I hear the fourth watch sounded from the drum tower.[19]
I must leave you, worthy wife, and go from the tent.
(The big gong is struck one . . . one. Ssu Lang makes a movement to go but his wife flings herself on her knees to restrain him and is dragged to the front stage. The big gong is struck. His wife begins to sing in san-pan time.)

MENG SHIH FU JEN:

I will not let go, husband.
If you want to leave, take me with you.
Ah, my husband.
(The big gong is beaten in tattoo. Ssu Lang sings.)

SSU LANG: Why do you pull me so urgently? *(The big gong is struck.)*

MENG SHIH FU JEN *(singing):* Our old mother is in the evening of her years and how can you push your wife aside?
(The big gong is beaten in tattoo. Ssu Lang sings.)

SSU LANG: How can I not know my old mother's advanced age. But I am like a boat in the middle of the river or a horse looking down from a cliff. I must thrust my wife away from me.
(The big gong is beaten in tattoo. Ssu Lang forcibly throws his wife to the ground and turning right goes towards the orchestra and thence to the exit. He turns his head to look at his wife. The big gong is struck and Ssu Lang cries out) Aiya!
(He stands with his legs straddled and supports his beard in his left hand, his right hand gestures towards his wife fainting on

19. The hours or watches of the night were beaten out on a drum placed in a special tower in old Chinese cities. There were five night watches of two hours between 7:00 P.M. and 5:00 A.M. Each watch was beaten out on the drum with the requisite number of strokes. The fifth watch, i.e., 5:00 A.M., was the hour at which the emperor gave audience in the past, hence the significance of Ssu Lang returning by the fifth watch.

the ground. The big gong is struck. Ssu Lang cries out again)
Aiya!
(He turns his back to the orchestra and from there goes to the left side of his wife and stands with left leg straddled across her, his beard supported by his left hand. The big gong is struck one, one, one, one. He gives his wife three blows. She comes to and stands up. The big gong is beaten. The two make an entrance together. Ssu Lang's wife kneels and the big gong is struck one . . . one . . . one. With his right hand Ssu Lang pulls his wife by the left hand. She is on her knees and is dragged in this position towards the exit. Ssu Lang gradually uses strength to pull her up. The big gong is struck. With his left hand Ssu Lang pulls and with his right hand forces apart, raising his left leg. At the same time his wife stands up, places her twisted left sleeve behind her at waist height and flings her right sleeve above her head to hang down at the rear. Together they face the exit standing apart. The big gong is struck, and they go off together.)

Scene 10

The big gong is struck in tattoo. Eighth and ninth sisters, followed by Yang Yen-chao come on and stand at the entry. After them comes the old mother who goes to front stage and sings in yao-pan time.

T'AI CHÜN:
About to seat myself in the rear tent
(The big gong is struck and the old woman makes a slight turn and sits on the left hand chair.)
Again I hear husband and wife weeping.
(The big gong is struck. Ssu Lang, his left hand holding his sash, luan tai, enters and going to front stage mimes his entry. He sings in yao-pan time.)
SSU LANG: I will take leave of my old mother and return to the northern outpost.
(The big gong is struck quickly and forcefully. He turns his body with his left leg forward as though to return through the door. His wife who enters the stage after Ssu Lang goes to

front stage and mimes going through the door. She caresses Ssu Lang. The big gong is struck in tattoo. Ssu Lang's wife begins to sing in san-pan time.)

MENG SHIH FU JEN: I'll discuss the matter again with my mother-in-law. *(Speaking.)* Aiya, mother-in-law, he has only just returned home and he wants to go back to the foreign state.

T'AI CHÜN: Aiya, my son! You have only just come back. Why do you want to return? Do you not know that to put filial loyalty first is the greatest thing in heaven and on earth?

(The big gong is struck. Ssu Lang calls out in distress.)

SSU LANG: Aiya, my mother. Does your son not know that the greatest thing in heaven and on earth is to put filial loyalty first. If I do not return by the fifth watch at dawn your foreign daughter-in-law and her child will be beheaded. *(The big gong is struck.)*

It is truly bitter. *(The big gong is beaten in tattoo.)*

T'AI CHÜN *(sings through her tears):* I weep, weep for my son Yen-hui.

SSU LANG *(facing his mother, sings):* My old mother. *(The big gong is struck.)*

YANG YEN-CHAO *(sings):* My fourth elder brother.

SSU LANG *(sings):* My worthy sixth brother.

EIGHTH AND NINTH SISTERS *(sing):* Our fourth elder brother. *(The big gong is struck.)*

SSU LANG *(sings):* Ah, my two kind sisters . . . *(The big gong is struck.)*

MENG SHIH FU JEN *(sings):* Hardhearted husband. *(The big gong is struck.)*

SSU LANG *(turns towards his wife and sings):* My unfortunate wife. *(The big gong is struck.)*

ALL: Ai . . . .

SSU LANG *(sings):* Mother, your son . . .

T'AI CHÜN *(sings):* My son . . .

YANG YEN-CHAO AND THE TWO SISTERS *(sing together):* Fourth elder brother.

MENG SHIH FU JEN *(sings):* My husband . . .

(Five beats of the large drum are heard from the orchestra. Ssu Lang counts the beats with the fingers of his right hand.

The big gong is beaten in tattoo. Ssu Lang goes to the rear of the stage, seats himself, and sings.)

SSU LANG: Aiya.

(The big gong is beaten swiftly and forcibly. Ssu Lang stands up, makes a salutation towards his old mother and turns to leave. He sings in san-pan time.)
The fifth watch has struck in the drum tower.
(The big gong is struck.)
I bid good-bye to my family
I must leave the tent.
(The big gong is struck one . . . one. Ssu Lang goes to front stage and places his left leg forward as if to go. Yang Yen-chao kneels on his left leg. Ssu Lang's wife kneels at the right. Ssu Lang places both hands on the shoulders of the eighth and ninth sisters. The big gong is beaten in tattoo. Ssu Lang sings in hsi-p'i yao-pan time.)

SSU LANG: I Yang Ssu Lang feel my heart pierced as by a knife.
(The old mother stands behind at the right and speaks through her tears.)

T'AI CHÜN: Ai, my son.

SSU LANG *(sings):*
I am unable to stay,
Old mother advanced in years . . .

YANG YEN-CHAO: Fourth elder brother.

SSU LANG *(sings):* I am unable to stay, worthy sixth brother with your great talents.

EIGHTH AND NINTH SISTERS *(speaking one after the other):* Fourth elder brother.

SSU LANG: I am loth to leave my worthy sisters not yet married.

MENG SHIH FU JEN: Cruelhearted husband.

SSU LANG: I am loth to leave my first wife. We must part. I Yang Ssu Lang am resolved in my mind to return to the foreign outpost. I must not delay but leave the whole family and go from this tent.
(The big gong is struck. The posing group divides. Ssu Lang goes through the entrance and towards the stage exit. The old mother goes front stage. Ssu Lang receives his sword and arrow of command and holds them under his left arm. He salutes Yang Yen-chao, who returns through the entrance to

*his original position. The big gong is struck. Ssu Lang mimes
reining in his horse with his right hand and turns left. He raises
his left leg, faces the stage exit. The big gong is struck. He
goes off. The old mother sings in yao-pan time.)*

T'AI CHÜN: When I see my son returning to the northern outpost
my old heart is filled with pain. Lead the way for me, eighth
and ninth sisters, no one knows if he will ever return.
(The big gong is beaten. She goes off.)

Scene 11

*The big gong is beaten. A groom comes on through the stage
exit and stands at the side of the stage as though dozing. Ssu
Lang comes on, in his left hand his sword and arrow of command. He goes front stage, turns right, and looks towards
the stage entry. He then turns to look at the groom, goes towards him, and rouses him. The groom awakens and goes to
front stage. He takes Ssu Lang's ma-pien, or riding switch
and both men mime dismounting a horse. The big gong is
struck. The two men go off.*

Scene 12

*Four lung-t'ao come on and stand at the entry. The two kuo-
chiu come on and go front stage. The first one speaks.*

FIRST KUO CHIU: His Highness fled through the pass.

SECOND KUO CHIU: We are implicated.

FIRST KUO CHIU: We've been deprived of our ranks.

SECOND KUO CHIU: Our salaries for the next three years.

FIRST KUO CHIU: Since His Highness stole the arrow of command
and fled through the pass, the Empress Dowager has been
very angry and taken away all our honors and titles. What's
to be done?

SECOND KUO CHIU: We'd better go to the gate of the pass and wait.

FIRST KUO CHIU: All right. Lead the way to the pass.

*(The big gong is beaten in tattoo. The two kuo-chiu follow the
lung-t'ao. The groom leads Ssu Lang on and they go to the*

front stage. The big gong is beaten. The two kuo-chiu raise their hands and cry out.)

BOTH KUO CHIU: Dismount, dismount.

(Ssu Lang turns right and dismounts. He gives his switch to the groom and goes to front stage. The first kuo-chiu strikes him and as Ssu Lang turns to avoid the blow the second kuo-chiu appears at the right and seizing Ssu Lang manacles him. The big gong is beaten. The two kuo-chiu lead Ssu Lang off; the four lung-t'ao and the groom follow.)

Scene 13

The big gong is struck. Four lung-t'ao come on and stand at the entrance. The Empress Dowager comes on and goes front stage. She speaks.

EMPRESS DOWAGER:

The eagle flew away.

(The big gong is beaten one, one, one.)

The swallow will be caught.

(The big gong is struck. She makes a wide turn and seats herself behind the table. The first kuo-chiu comes on, goes front stage and mimes making an entry. Inside the palace he makes a salutation.)

FIRST KUO CHIU: Mu I has been arrested!

EMPRESS DOWAGER *(speaks):* Bring him in.

(The kuo-chiu goes to front stage and calls out. The big gong is struck. Ssu Lang comes on and goes front stage. He is manacled and followed by the second kuo-chiu who stands to his left.)

SSU LANG *(sings k'uai-pan time):* I am terrified when I suddenly hear the Empress Dowager's order of arrest. It's as though two of my three souls had departed. I'll stride into the Silver Hall *(The big gong is beaten quickly and forcefully. The second kuo-chiu leads Ssu Lang to report. Ssu Lang goes to center stage and begins to sing in san-pan time.)* and confess my crime to the Empress before the seat of justice. *(The big gong is struck.)*

EMPRESS DOWAGER *(sings):* When I see Mu I, anger springs from

my heart. Why did you dare to cheat me? Tell me the truth
from beginning to end. Where is your family home and your
state?

SSU LANG *(sings):*

My home was in T'zu-chou.

Huo T'ang Chai was my house.

My father was a top-ranking official.

Her excellency my mother was named She.

Empress, you ask my names

I am Yang.

*(The big gong is struck one . . . one . . . one. The Empress
Dowager bangs angrily on the table with her right hand.)*

EMPRESS DOWAGER: Yang what?

BOTH KUO CHIU *(crying in unison):* Speak!

(Ssu Lang turns left and begins to sing.)

SSU LANG: Ssu Lang Yen-hui is your son-in-law's name.

EMPRESS DOWAGER *(calling angrily):* T'u! *(The big gong is struck.
The Empress sings in k'uai-pan time.)* I shout for the executioners from both sides. Take him out of the Silver Hall and
behead him! *(The big gong is struck.)*

SSU LANG *(speaks):* Aiya. *(He goes to the nine dragons' mouth and
begins to sing in yao-pan time.)*

If I had known earlier today that I'd lose my life

(The big gong is struck once.)

I should not have returned from visiting my mother.

Looking towards the rear palace, I cry out Princess.

(He goes front stage and sings a verse in san-pan time.)

If I can see my wife I'll die at ease.

*(He sits on a chair. The Princess is led on by one of the kuo-
chiu. She goes to front stage and sings in liu-shui-pan time.)*

PRINCESS: Suddenly I hear a palace official who has come to report
that my husband has been arrested. *(She changes to san-pan
time.)* What order has he violated? *(As she sings she goes to
the right of Ssu Lang. There she calls out)* Husband! *(The big
gong is beaten in tattoo. The Princess sings again.)* Why are
you bound as though for execution . . .

SSU LANG *(sings in tao-pan time):* A little while ago they bound me
up. I am confused, I cannot make it out. *(The big gong is*

struck one . . . one. Ssu Lang turns left in his seat.) Ah, Princess!

FIRST KUO CHIU *(speaks):* I speak for your mother. Which side are you on, Princess?

PRINCESS *(speaks):* I am on this side. *(The big gong is struck.)*

SSU LANG *(stands up and sings):* I see the Princess in front. Keep your tears and if you remember what a faithful wife should do, go quickly to the Silver Hall and intercede for me, Yang Ssu Lang, the man you married. *(Ssu Lang sits once more. The big gong is struck . . . one . . . one. The Princess speaks.)*

PRINCESS: Husband. *(The big gong is struck in tattoo. The Princess sings in liu-shui-pan time.)* Husband, bear your bonds a little while. I will go to the Palace and intercede for you. Taking my pretty child in my arms, I enter the Silver Hall.

(The big gong is beaten. The Princess turns right, mimes entering a door and goes to the right where she sings.)

PRINCESS: If they question me, I shall reply.

(The big gong is beaten in tattoo. The Empress Dowager sings in san-pan time.)

EMPRESS DOWAGER:

Daughter, why do you not remain in your own quarters?

What circumstances bring you to the Silver Hall?

For what reason are you here?

PRINCESS:

His Highness my husband is bound up for execution.

What has he done wrong?

(The big gong is beaten in tattoo.)

EMPRESS DOWAGER:

The pair of you stole my arrow of command.

Have you not got matters the wrong way round,

Coming to question me, your mother?

(The big gong is beaten in tattoo.)

PRINCESS: His Highness has incurred punishment and ought to be executed, but spare him for my sake.

EMPRESS DOWAGER: He will most certainly be executed. I refuse to pardon him. *(The big gong is struck. The Empress Dowager bangs the table with a wooden baton.)*

PRINCESS *(cries out):* Ya!

(The big gong is struck. The Princess makes a salutation and

begins to sing in liu-shui-pan time.) My Empress mother will grant no reprieve. I don't know what to do. I must leave the Silver Hall and ask His Highness what to do.
(The big gong is beaten one . . . one . . . one. She speaks)
Husband. *(The big gong is beaten in tattoo. The Princess sings san-pan time.)* Together we must implore our mother.
(The big gong is struck. Ssu Lang stands and with the Princess enters the door and kneels before the Empress Dowager.)

SSU LANG *(cries out):* Empress Dowager.

PRINCESS *(cries out):* Ah, mother.

SSU LANG *(cries out):* Ah, Empress Dowager—ya. *(The big gong is struck. Ssu Lang sings through his tears.)*
I weep
(The big gong is struck one . . . one . . . one.)
I weep before you, venerable Empress Dowager—ah.

PRINCESS *(sings):*
I call out.
(The big gong is beaten in tattoo.)
I call out before you, your child, my mother.

SSU LANG *(sings):*
I should have been beheaded at the beginning when I was captured.
(The big gong is struck once.)

PRINCESS *(sings):*
You should not have married me to him.
Then it would not have mattered.
(The big gong is struck once.)
Whom shall I rely on later in life?
(The big gong is struck once.)

SSU LANG *(sings):* Venerable Empress Dowager—ah. *(The big gong is struck one . . . one . . . one.)*

PRINCESS *(sings):* My venerable mother. *(The big gong is struck.)*

SSU LANG AND PRINCESS *(together):* Ah. *(The big gong is beaten. The hu-ch'in stops playing.)*

SSU LANG *(sings without accompaniment):* My mother-in-law. *(The big gong is struck. The Empress Dowager takes her wooden baton and strikes the table with it.)*

EMPRESS DOWAGER: You ought to be ashamed.
(The two kuo-chiu go to the front stage to consult.)

FIRST KUO CHIU: Take a look. The two young people are weeping piteously; let's go and intercede for them.

SECOND KUO CHIU: I think it's no good asking her.

FIRST KUO CHIU: The Empress Dowager likes me. I'll go in, two or three words and I'll guarantee I'll be able to fix it for him.

SECOND KUO CHIU: She'll eat you.

(The two turn, go forward towards the Empress, and kneel before her.)

BOTH KUO CHIU: We two k'ou-t'ou before you, Empress Dowager.

EMPRESS DOWAGER *(speaks):* I say, you two, why are you kneeling down there before me, what's the matter?

BOTH KUO CHIU *(together):* Mu I committed a crime and deserves to be executed but please pardon him for our sakes.

EMPRESS DOWAGER: What, you two dare to talk about pardoning Mu I?

BOTH KUO CHIU *(together):* Not dare to talk about, but to ask the Empress Dowager to show mercy.

EMPRESS DOWAGER *(speaks):* Let me ask you something. When Mu I first went through the pass, it was you two who allowed him to go?

BOTH KUO CHIU *(in unison):* He did, he did.

EMPRESS DOWAGER: Oh, he did and when he came back, who arrested him?

BOTH KUO CHIU *(together):* I did, I did, I did!

EMPRESS DOWAGER: Oh, you did. *(She smiles. The two kuo-chiu stand up.)* Ah.

BOTH KUO CHIU: I say, Empress Dowager, you like me.

(The Empress bangs on the table with her wooden baton.)

EMPRESS DOWAGER: Enough! *(The big gong is beaten. The two kuo-chiu go down on their knees. The Empress speaks)* You two allowed Mu I to commit a crime. I'll execute him first and afterwards I'll demand your heads.

(The big gong is struck. The Empress Dowager strikes the table and the two kuo-chiu rise and go to the front of the stage and speak together.)

BOTH KUO CHIU: I say, this doesn't make sense, does it.

PRINCESS *(cries out):* Ya. *(The big gong is beaten in tattoo. The Princess stands up and sings in liu-shui-pan time.)*

She will not listen to them or to me. It would have been better had he been executed when he was first captured.

EMPRESS DOWAGER *(sings):* I didn't know he was a Yang then.

PRINCESS *(sings):* If you behead His Highness, your daughter will have no one to rely on.

EMPRESS DOWAGER *(sings):* I'll find you another bridegroom.

PRINCESS *(sings):* A good horse cannot wear two saddles.

EMPRESS DOWAGER *(sings):* That one . . . *(The big gong is struck one . . . one . . . one.)* will never have a long life or live to be an old man. *(The Empress speaks)* Leave the Hall.

PRINCESS *(speaks):* Ya! *(The big gong is beaten. The Princess goes out of the door and sings in san-pan time.)* In the Silver Hall I find no solution . . .
(The large gong is struck once. The hu-ch'in plays a hsiao kuo-men. The two kuo-chiu speak in unison.)

BOTH KUO CHIU: I say, Princess. Why are you still singing drama at a time like this? Think of a way out quickly.

PRINCESS: I simply do not know how to deal with these matters. Do you two have any good ideas?

BOTH KUO CHIU *(in unison):* I should like to ask you a question. Whom did you use to steal the mandate arrow?

PRINCESS: Whom did I use? Why A Ko of course.

BOTH KUO CHIU *(in unison):* Well, can't you use A Ko again?

PRINCESS: What? How can I do that?

BOTH KUO CHIU *(in unison):* Let me tell you. Take A Ko before the Empress Dowager, toss him into her lap, seize a sword, cry out, "I had better die," and pretend to cut your throat. The Empress Dowager will then take pity on her grandson and pardon his father.

PRINCESS: What? Toss my baby to my mother and pretend to cut my throat with a sword?

BOTH KUO CHIU: That's right. But only pretend, you know, don't really cut your throat.

PRINCESS: Oh, I can't do it, I can't do it.

BOTH KUO CHIU: Why can't you do it?

PRINCESS: How can I threaten A Ko? I cannot abandon my child.

FIRST KUO CHIU: You are very foolish, if you give up the little one . . .

SECOND KUO CHIU: . . . then you save the big one . . .

FIRST KUO CHIU: . . . if you don't want to give up the little one . . .

SECOND KUO CHIU: . . . then how can you save the big one . . .

FIRST KUO CHIU: . . . if you save the big one . . .

SECOND KUO CHIU: . . . in the future there will be lots of new little ones.

PRINCESS: Oh, stop talking rubbish but let me try.

BOTH KUO CHIU *(in unison):* Good. You try it then.

PRINCESS *(crying out):* Ai-i-i *(The large gong is beaten and the Princess begins to sing in san-pan time.)* A Ko shall be thrown to my mother.

(There are two light beats on the big gong and then a loud and long one. The Princess walks towards the table with her child and hurls it at the Empress, then she seizes a sword at the side of the throne, and speaks) I cannot continue to live, I am going to commit suicide, I am going to commit suicide, I must die.

(The two kuo-chiu pretend to try stop her and she sinks to the floor weeping.)

EMPRESS DOWAGER *(speaks):* Calm yourself, calm yourself. I'll reprieve him.

BOTH KUO CHIU *(in unison):* Don't make any more fuss, the Empress Dowager's reprieved him.

PRINCESS *(sits up on the floor smiling):* What? Reprieved?

BOTH KUO CHIU *(in unison):* Reprieved!

PRINCESS *(stands up and speaks):* Then I needn't die.

BOTH KUO CHIU: Did you intend to die in the first place?

EMPRESS DOWAGER *(speaks):* Prince go and change your clothes!

(The big gong is struck. The two kuo-chiu go towards Ssu Lang intending to remove his handcuffs but the Princess quickly stops them.)

PRINCESS: Don't you touch him, your hands are too dirty.

(Ssu Lang stands up and the Princess frees him from the handcuffs and gives them to a stage hand. Ssu Lang bows his head and goes towards the stage entry but is stopped by the second kuo-chiu.)

SECOND KUO CHIU: Hey, you're going the wrong way, your insignificant quarters are over at that frontier.

(Ssu Lang turns left, walks slowly towards the exit and goes off. The Princess turns her head to look at her mother from

*the frontstage where she has placed herself, then towards the
two kuo-chiu.)*

PRINCESS *(speaks):* I say you two, the Empress Dowager has re-
lented but she is still angry and she has not handed A Ko back.
What shall I do?

BOTH KUO CHIU *(in unison):* That's not difficult. When you were a
child you could get round your mother when she was angry,
give the Empress Dowager a special salute as you did then.

PRINCESS: Will it succeed?

BOTH KUO CHIU: It will succeed.

PRINCESS: Let's try. *(She turns to the right and stands at the right
side of the table from the Empress Dowager. She speaks)* I
say Mother, my husband was at fault just now but don't be
angry, I will salute you on his behalf.

*(She curtseys. The big gong is struck once. The Empress Dowa-
ger turns her head away and will not look at her daughter.)*

BOTH KUO CHIU *(in unison):* The old coat has lost its surface.

(The Princess slowly goes to the front of the stage.)

PRINCESS: It's no good.

BOTH KUO CHIU: This time it's no good but try once again.

PRINCESS: Shall I try?

BOTH KUO CHIU *(in unison):* This time it will work.

PRINCESS: All right, I'll try once more.

BOTH KUO CHIU: We'll watch you.

*(The Princess turns left and walks towards the left side of the
table and speaks to her mother.)*

PRINCESS: I say, Mother, it was all my fault just now, I did not mean
to offend you. We pay you our respects and make our apolo-
gies.

*(The big gong is beaten once. The Empress Dowager peevishly
turns to the right.)*

BOTH KUO CHIU *(in unison):* The crane must strut on the roof beam.

*(The Princess with a disappointed look goes slowly to the
front stage and speaks to the two kuo-chiu.)*

PRINCESS: It's still no use.

BOTH KUO CHIU: Third time lucky! Twice you failed by taking two
candles. This time try an incense burner.

PRINCESS: I'm finished. Don't direct me any more, my legs are tired.

BOTH KUO CHIU: This time you will certainly succeed.

PRINCESS: Really succeed?

BOTH KUO CHIU: Really succeed.

(The Princess goes to the middle of the stage and speaks.)

PRINCESS: I say, Mother, don't be angry. We cannot bear to give you distress. Please return A Ko to us and we pay you our respects once more.

(The large gong is beaten once. The Princess curtseys and the Empress Dowager breaks into a smile.)

BOTH KUO CHIU *(in unison):* That's it. She's smiled!

(The Empress Dowager takes A Ko and gives him to the Princess.)

EMPRESS DOWAGER: Call my son-in-law.

(The Princess stands to the right after taking the child.)

BOTH KUO CHIU *(in unison):* Son-in-law, come here

(The big gong is heard in a brisk passage. Ssu Lang enters from the exit side of the stage. He has changed his clothes and he begins to sing in liu-shui-pan time.)

SSU LANG:

Just now I traveled out in defiance of the law

Many thanks to you, Princess, for liberating me.

Before thanking the Empress Dowager

(Sings san-pan time.)

I first thank you.

(One beat on the large gong, a pause, one beat, a pause, one long beat. The hu-ch'in plays. He speaks.)

Just now I was a criminal.

Many thanks to you Princess for speaking on my behalf.

I stand here and thank you.

(Both hands clasped, he salutes her.)

PRINCESS: I do not deserve such thanks.

SSU LANG *(speaks):* I must thank you once again. *(He takes one step forward and again salutes her.)*

PRINCESS: I do not deserve such thanks.

SSU LANG *(speaks):* I must thank you once again. *(He takes one step forward and again salutes her.)*

PRINCESS *(she returns the salute):* I do not deserve it.

SSU LANG: According to principles of respect and reverence I must thank you. *(He takes one more step forward and makes a salute.)*

PRINCESS *(returning the salute):* I do not deserve it.

SSU LANG *(speaks):* Princess . . . . *(The big gong is struck and Ssu Lang begins to sing in san-pan time.)* My mother described you as virtuous and fine. *(The big gong is struck one, one, one.)*

PRINCESS *(sits and speaks):* Husband . . . . *(The big gong is struck. She sings in san-man pan time.)* My Empress mother offended you, I ask your pardon. *(The big gong is struck one, one, one. The hu-ch'in plays. She speaks)* Husband, just now it was only my Empress mother who offended you, I pay my respects to you. *(She steps forward and salutes him.)*

SSU LANG: I do not deserve it.

PRINCESS: I apologize to you. *(She takes another step forward and salutes him.)*

SSU LANG *(speaks):* Really, I do not deserve it. *(The big gong is struck.)*

PRINCESS *(sings in san-pan time):* Husband, do not bother to mention it at all. *(The big gong is struck.)*

SSU LANG: Husband and wife together enter the Silver Hall. *(The big gong is struck. The two go indoors, Ssu Lang to the left and the Princess to the right. This action is, of course, mimed, there is no actual door and all the actors are on the stage together. Ssu Lang and the Princess kneel before the Empress Dowager. He sings san-pan time.)* I earnestly thank you for not executing me, Empress mother.

EMPRESS DOWAGER *(taking up the arrow of command, speaks):* Imperial son-in-law, listen to my order. *(The big gong is struck one, two, pause and one.)*

SSU LANG *(speaks):* I am listening.

EMPRESS DOWAGER: I bestow on you this arrow of command and order you to guard the Pei T'ien Gate. This time do your official work well. If you want to go again to visit your mother's camp in private, watch out for your head. *(The Empress raps the table with a wooden striker.)* I have finished.

(The lung-t'ao with the two kuo-chiu walk round and go to the exit where they stand as the Empress Dowager comes out from behind the table (her audience throne) where she has been seated.)

SSU LANG: I will obey your command.

(The Princess and Ssu Lang stand up together and hold each other by the arms. A groom enters from the exit side of the stage. Ssu Lang turns right, the Princess left.)

PRINCESS *(speaks):* Did you hear what was said? My Empress mother has given you an order and told you to guard the Pei T'ien Gate. You must do your work well and if you wish to visit your mother again without telling anyone don't forget to take the arrow of command. *(The words, "visit your mother" in Chinese are a play on the title of the play which is often abbreviated by playgoers to T'an Mu.)*

(The big gong is struck once, twice, pause, once. The Princess turns to the left and Ssu Lang makes a salutation and turns to face the audience.)

SSU LANG *(speaks):* Bring my horse, I go to the Pei T'ien Gate.

(The big gong is struck in a vigorous passage. The groom comes to front stage holding the ma-pien or riding switch which symbolizes a horse. Ssu Lang takes the switch, goes through the pantomime of mounting a horse, then both sweep off the stage.)

THE END

The Butterfly Dream

Hu Tieh Meng, ching-hsi
A traditional Peking play

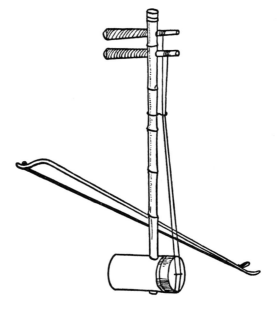

Persons in the Play

CHUANG TZU, a Taoist scholar and sorcerer (a sheng role)
T'IEN SHIH, the coquettish wife of Chuang Tzu (a hua-tan role)
HUA SHEN (a spirit), the spirit of Chuang Tzu transformed into a
  handsome young man (a hsiao-sheng role)
TUNG ERH (a boy), servant boy to T'ien Shih (a ch'ou role)
ERH PAI WU ("Two hundred and fifty"), a paper boy used as a
  funeral effigy (a ch'ou role)
T'UNG NÜ (a paper girl), supernumerary.

There are three scenes in the Chinese original and there is one curtain, a scene changing device with action in front of the curtain. The
action takes place outside the home of Chuang Tzu, in the living
quarters of his house, and in his funeral chamber. The time is the
period of the Warring States (481–221 B.C.).

The Story of the Play

The Butterfly Dream was really a part of a much longer play first performed in the Soochow, k'un-ch'ü, style during the Ming dynasty (A.D. 1368–1644). The act from which it is taken was called *P'i Kuan*, "Breaking Open the Coffin," an alternative title which has been commonly used for the present play. This play should not be confused with another one also entitled *The Butterfly Dream* but written by the Yuan dramatist Kuan Han-ch'ing during the thirteenth century and having a totally different theme. The present play derived its plot from a Ming novel and there have been several versions during its long history but the "Breaking Open the Coffin" scene was the only one that survived for active performance on the stage. The version on which this translation is based was first staged as ching-hsi or Peking-style theater during the last years of the nineteenth century and has more or less retained its form through later decades.

The action of the plot is set in the Warring States (481–221 B.C.), but like *Ssu Lang Visits His Mother* and all traditional drama, there is no attempt at historical accuracy; the only considerations are for stage effect. *The Butterfly Dream*, a satirical comedy on the inconstancy of woman, is devised primarily as a vehicle for the hua-tan or coquettish female role; however, the part of Erh Pai Wu, "Two hundred and fifty," provides ample scope for the mime and comic business of the Chinese clown. Singing is at a minimum in this play; the emphasis is on movement and expression.

The play has always been a favorite item in the main programs

95

of the large theaters, while it was rare to visit the small teahouse theaters of Nanking and Shanghai and not find *The Butterfly Dream* being staged on some evening during the week. It was a useful display piece for the actresses who rose to prominence during the thirties and forties to show their talents as stage coquettes, for this play demands great technical competence. After 1949, *The Butterfly Dream* was frowned upon by the arbiters of Marxist dramatic taste, ceased to be performed in the large theaters, and finally disappeared from the boards completely. In one revised version of the early post-1949 era, T'ien Shih, instead of administering her *coup de grâce* with the ax, threw it down, leapt to her feet, and exclaimed to the audience that she refused to kill herself as this was the New Society where wives now had equal status.

The action of the play commences as Chuang Tzu, a Taoist scholar-magician, returns from retreat in the mountains for a reunion with his pretty and coquettish wife, T'ien Shih. On the way home he comes across a young woman furiously fanning the earth on a newly made grave. In answer to his surprised questioning, Chuang Tzu is told that the widow's husband had loved her dearly and begged her not to marry again before the earth on his grave was dry. Moved by her tears Chuang Tzu quickly dries the grave by virtue of his magic powers and, as a token of gratitude, is presented with the widow's fan. On it she inscribes this message: "Taoist traveler who pitied me, when you return home tell your wife that she would be no more virtuous than I have been."

Chuang Tzu's wife is furious when her husband tells his story and shows her the fan. She cries that no decent woman would behave like the widow and reaffirms her eternal fidelity to Chuang Tzu. He by now is thoroughly skeptical of all wifely vows and decides to test T'ien Shih's constancy by a magic ruse. He pretends to die, an event which provides good comic business when the servant goes out to buy a coffin and arrange for the funeral rituals. Chuang Tzu then turns into a handsome young scholar arrived to mourn his dead teacher. He is accompanied by his servant, a paper effigy from his own funeral paraphernalia whom he has brought to life by his magic powers. T'ien Shih immediately falls in love with the handsome stranger and, though still in mourning for her "dead" husband, arranges a wedding on the spot to the great disgust of the servant, grief-stricken through the sudden loss of his master.

On the night of the bridal ceremony the new "husband" is suddenly seized with a mortal illness under the direction of the "departed" Chuang Tzu, and the disappointed T'ien Shih is told by her new lover's servant that the only way to bring his master back to the world of the living is by administering a drug concocted from the brain of a newly dead person. Overcome by her amorous passion, T'ien Shih's first thought is to kill the servant boy but he realizes her intentions and flinging off his livery flees the house. Unable to restrain her longings T'ien Shih next steels herself to break open her "dead" husband's coffin and procure the necessary ingredient to save her lover. After emotional preparations she takes an ax and sets about her gruesome task only to be confronted by the wrathful figure of her former husband now very much alive. He accuses his wife of adultery but she is defiant and calls upon him to prove his accusations. Chuang Tzu thereupon recalls the form of the handsome stranger who vanishes again beneath the agonized embrace of T'ien Shih. In her mortification T'ien Shih seizes her ax and kills herself on the spot as Chuang Tzu with mocking laughter leaves the house for ever.

Costumes Worn by
the Characters in the Play

T'IEN SHIH (a hua-tan role)

T'ien Shih has five changes of costume during the course of the play. First she appears wearing informal costume that is suggestive of a coquette's amorous character according to Chinese stage conventions. The second change of costume represents the formal costume of a lady at home; the third change represents mourning dress; the fourth change bridal dress, and the last change represents that of an abandoned woman attired for the gruesome manual labor she has decided upon. The basic hair style throughout is the *ta-t'ou* (see p. 29). Different accessories in the form of decorations and jewelry are added or taken away according to the needs of the particular scene T'ien Shih is dressed for but the basic coiffure remains unchanged.

When she first appears T'ien Shih wears an *ao* with a skirt, *hsiu-hua ch'ün tzu*. The ao is a waist-length tunic with a high collar; it fastens across the right breast to the armpit and then down the side. The wide sleeves are bracelet length without any "water sleeves." The long skirt which covers the feet is a wrap over type fastened round the waist with tapes. It is pleated and has a rectangular embroidered panel down the front. The ao is worn by women of a coquettish nature and it is a typical garment for the hua-tan role. It is also worn as costume for a maidservant who is frequently an important character type portrayed through the hua-tan technique.

The ao is usually worn with trousers, *k'u-tzu*, but as T'ien Shih is a married woman, who is never portrayed wearing trousers, and the wife of a scholar as well, the costume she wears strikes a happy medium in stage symbolism. The entire costume is made of richly embroidered and flowered satin with red as the predominating color. The shoes worn are the *ts'ai hsüeh*, flat-soled slippers of embroidered silk to match the costume with a large tassel on the toe of each shoe.

For her second change of costume, T'ien Shih is in formal attire to greet her husband. She wears a similar skirt and shoes to the ensemble described above but the upper garment is what is called a *shih-shih hsüeh-tzu*. It is made of soft satin, knee length, open down the center with a slit at either side, with a high collar and long "water sleeves." The predominating color of this outfit is a rich blue.

For her third change of costume T'ien Shih is completely in white, the color for mourning in China. Her total costume is very similar to the one previously described apart from color and pattern. The upper garment is called *nü hsiao-i* and together with the panels of the skirt has a delicately embroidered border pattern in blue. It is made of white satin and has long "water sleeves." A large white silk scarf is worn over the coiffure like a hood and knotted to hang down the back to below the waist. Her shoes are the ts'ai hsüeh described previously, but in matching white silk.

T'ien Shih wears a complete bridal outfit in the fourth change of costume; it is more or less identical in style with the formal costume worn in the second change but the heavily embroidered satin garment is crimson in color, crimson being the color for marriage and celebration.

In her final change for the "Breaking Open the Coffin" scene she wears a *pu ao*, a plain tunic of the same cut and style as the one worn in the first scene but made of plain crimson cotton and entirely unadorned in any way. A broad white sash is knotted round the waist of the tunic and wide black cotton trousers and simple black cotton slippers complete the costume. In this scene all jewelry and ornaments have been removed from T'ien Shih's hair and a long switch of hair has been released from the chignon at the back of her coiffure to hang down the left side of the face. This switch she holds between her teeth in the moments of agitation which mark the final scene. Although the other costumes worn by T'ien Shih in general style and form may be seen worn in other plays, the one worn in the final scene is unique to this play as is the style of mourning costume worn for the funeral chamber scene.

TUNG ERH (the servant boy, a ch'ou role)

The servant boy in the first part of the play wears a *ch'a-i*, a loose waist-length tunic of plain blue cotton cloth with wide sleeves and short "water sleeves" of white silk attached to the cuffs. It usually has an open crossover neck with a broad black border of several inches width; the garment fastens under the right armpit and down the side. A white crossover silk stock is worn around the neck with this costume. In this play the ch'a-i, which is always worn by servants and similar characters, is a variation on the strictly orthodox version, for it has a neckline modeled on a similar garment, the *an erh-i*, used for a child character. This garment fastens down the front with a tape at the base of the neck opening which has a broad white border. This costume is usually made of silk. The one worn by the servant boy in this play, however, although opening down the front, has a simple plain black border round the neck opening and, as already noted, is made of cotton cloth. It is, therefore, a compromise between a servant's and a child's costume and symbolizes the character concerned, who is a servant and an impudent young boy at the same time. Around the waist of the tunic the servant boy wears a white pleated skirt or *ch'ün-tzu* of the type worn by the ch'ing-i characters. It is folded double to give a bunched-up effect and symbolizes an apron. This costume is an example of how stage garments are interchangeable for special purposes. The rest of the servant boy's costume consists of wide black cotton trousers, white cotton stockings, and plain black cotton slippers. Sometimes the comic actors wear their trousers tucked into these stockings to give a leggings-knickerbocker effect. Around his head the servant boy wears a narrow cloth bandeau with a bow and a dangling tassel at either side. This headdress is worn by the comic actors to symbolize a child or young boy. Sometimes it is nothing more than a simple broad black tape taken round the head and knotted to hang down at the left.

In his second change of costume the servant boy changes his tunic and "apron" for a simple white cotton three-quarter length garment, *hsiao-i.* This has turned up cuffs (*ma-t'i hsiu*) rather than "water sleeves," no collar, opens down the front, and is bound round the waist with a thin white tape. In his hand the servant carries a long switch made of bamboo and white paper representing a feather duster. The rest of the costume remains unchanged from the previous scene although there can be variations on this mourning costume which the comic actors are free to adapt to some extent, using the mourning dress to emphasize their own white make-up and appearing completely in white from head to foot with a white kerchief bound round the head. The form described here, however, is the more traditional style.

CHUANG TZU (a sheng role)

Chuang Tzu has three changes of costume during the play. On his first appearance he wears a long satin robe, *hsieh-tzu*, which covers the feet and has an open crossover neck with the robe fastening across the chest under the right armpit. It has long wide sleeves with white silk "water sleeves" attached to the cuffs and is of a solid bronze color. A white silk crossover stock is worn round the neck of the actor. Over the main robe a second garment called *pei-hsin* is added. This is a long satin robe without any sleeves, having splits at either side, opening down the front, and ornately embroidered in a flowered pattern over a rich olive green base. It represents an outdoor garment and symbolizes Chuang Tzu's returning from his mountain retreat. The hat worn with this costume is a soft embroidered cap with a high crown designed in a semistiff wedge shape. Technically known as *kao fang-chin*, it represents the hat of a scholar. Chuang Tzu wears a full black beard, *man-jan*, made of horsehair bound to a wire frame which fits over the ears and rests just above the mouth on the upper lip. Two long switches hang down from either ear and separate from the main sweep of the beard which is used with great effect in the gestural techniques used by Chuang Tzu in the course of the play.

In his hand Chuang Tzu carries a *ying ch'en*, a long plume of horsehair bound to a handle with a thong and derived from an actual article that was carried by Buddhist priests and known as a *fu-tzu*. It symbolized spiritual direction exercised by the priest and was a mark of religious authority as well as serving a more practical purpose as a fly switch — his creed forbade the priest to kill flies. On the Chinese stage is is frequently used as a sign of religious authority but is also used as a symbol for supernatural powers, a kind of magic wand, as in the case of Chuang Tzu. A small property, it is used to great effect in gesture techniques and in the dance parts of female characters.

In his second change of costume Chuang Tzu wears the *pa-kua* robe or *pa-kua i* which is only used by specific characters, notably Chu-Ko Liang in the Three Kingdom play cycle. It symbolizes the possession of special intellectual powers and supernatural talents. The robe derives its name from the *pa-kua* or Eight Diagrams, an arrangement of cabalistic signs in numerical pattern. These form the basis of the classic Canon of Changes which was a basis for divination and was regarded as containing the elements of metaphysical knowledge. The diagrams are in the shape of different length bars in specific formations and plaques. Showing them arranged round a central *yang* and *yin* motif, the traditional symbol of creation, was a talisman against misfortune in old China.

On Chuang Tzu's robe the yang and yin symbol is embroidered in heavy gold and silver thread on the front and back of the upper part of the garment with the eight diagrams also embroidered in heavy gold thread on the sleeves and lower part of the robe. The robe itself is slit at either side to the waist where there is an embroidered key pattern making the pattern of a girdle round the robe and wide borders to the slits. The two lower halves of the garment are apron-shaped and there are silk "water sleeves" attached to the cuffs. The robe has a high but soft embroidered collar which opens in crossover style at the front and fastens beneath the right armpit. The black beard is worn with this garment and traditionally the same kind of cap described previously except that it is decorated with an embroidered yang and yin symbol. Within recent times it has been customary for Chuang Tzu to wear a gold crown with an ornate forepiece decorated with *jung-ch'iu*, colored silk pompons, and this is worn over a black wig of loose hair hanging down Chuang Tzu's back. Traditionally he carries a fan in one hand and the *ying ch'en* or fly switch in the other. With the more ornate ensemble just described, the switch is replaced by a long wooden stave with a carved dragon head decorated with silk tassels. This costume of course represents the dress of a spirit transformed by supernatural powers.

In the final scene where Chuang Tzu springs to life in his coffin, he wears a simple black cotton *hsieh-tzu*, the style of robe described for the first scene. On his head he wears a *shuai-fa*, a long plume of black horsehair mounted on a short upright support fixed to the skullcap-like foundation which is used as the base for all kinds of headdresses. The shuai-fa is worn by ghosts, prisoners, and people in tragic circumstances.

HUA SHEN (a hsiao-sheng role)

The spirit representing T'ien Shih's handsome young lover wears a cap similar in shape to Chuang Tzu's but heavily embroidered to match his robe and decorated with a large brilliant above the brow. His robe, *hua ying hsieh-tzu*, is very similar to the garment worn by Chuang Tzu in cut, this being a standard costume form, but it is much more feminine in its decoration — sky blue satin decorated with large sprays of embroidered plum blossoms. It has long "water sleeves" which are "played" with great effect by the hsiao-sheng actor who takes this part. A fan is never absent from his hand in all his posturings. He wears embroidered slippers with felt soles an inch thick, the toes of the slippers being curved back in a decorated shape rather similar to the blunt prow of a galleon in miniature.

ERH PAI WU ("Two hundred and fifty," a ch'ou role)

The paper boy represents the effigy of a servant boy traditionally burned at a funeral in order that the dead man should be adequately attended in the spirit world. The costume in these days is made of stiff shiny plastic, turquoise blue or green in color, and has two parts consisting of a collarless robe, with wide sleeves (no "water sleeves," of course) slit at either side and cut calf length, and a sleeveless waistcoat of contrasting color, buttoning across from the neck opening and down the right front of the garment. The stiff material of which this garment is made emphasizes the angular puppet-like gait of the actor playing this role. Thick white cotton stockings in the form of leggings and black cotton flat-soled slippers make up the rest of the costume. The hat worn is the little round black satin cap known as the *kua-p'i mao* which is surmounted by a crimson silk corded button on the peak of the crown. At the rear of the cap a short queue or pigtail is attached standing out at right angles with the end sharply upturned again in a right angle. This costume is a kind of caricature of the ordinary formal style of the man in the street during the Ch'ing dynasty. A pair of white cotton gloves worn on the rigidly held hands of the paper boy add a somewhat more modern touch to the costume, although they were introduced as a measure against having the hands whitened to match the dead white of the facial make-up. Relieved only by the black penciled eyebrows and a large round crimson spot on either cheek, the facial make-up is a most uncharacteristic Chinese make-up and even suggests the influence of Western ballet doll make-up at some point. This is purely speculative, however, and the design is always used for the paper boy role.

The Butterfly Dream

Prelude to the first scene

The first scene of this play is preceded by a dream sequence which is performed solo by the actress playing T'ien Shih. It provides an opportunity for displaying the vivacious gesture language and mime technique traditionally associated with the hua-tan role. In this first entry only a few lines are spoken throughout by the actress; the rest is a pattern of graceful movement. The impression is skillfully conveyed of a lonely young woman pining for want of an absent husband and in her dreams imagining his physical presence with all its amorous implication until she is rudely brought back to earth by the sudden appearance of her servant boy. Following this she displays her true character as a coquette before disappearing from the stage prior to her husband's return. The appetite of the audience has now been whetted in anticipation of some interesting developments with the full knowledge that the heroine is more than capable of satisfying their expectations.

There is no house curtain to the stage which is completely bare of anything except a small rectangular wooden table draped with a richly embroidered crimson silk cloth and two simple wooden chairs similarly covered, one chair in front of the table and one behind. This furniture is placed directly against an embroidered silk curtain which hangs over the center of the simple black curtain that forms the rear of the stage and which has one opening at the right for entry and another at the left for exit.

The small gong is beaten in the orchestra and T'ien Shih enters from the right of the rear stage and walks towards the front. She carries a large silk kerchief in her hand, an indispensable small property of the hua-tan actress. Her steps are small and mincing,

105

the feet being kept parallel and separated by a distance of one inch. As she walks the heel is placed on the ground before the toes which on the first foot are only three inches ahead of the second with each step that is taken. The hands move from side to side across the waist of the moving actress. T'ien Shih stops at the front stage and assumes a pose — both hands are held to the right, the right hand being higher than the left, which is placed across the waist to gracefully support the kerchief grasped in the right hand. The right foot is placed behind the left. Her head is then tilted left with the right hand brought to her head as the whole body is inclined left with the right foot still behind the left. The position is then changed with the head tilted to the right and both hands brought across to the left as the left foot is placed behind the right foot. Then both hands are moved gracefully and gently towards the thighs with the head delicately tilted to the left. Next, both hands are raised to the left, grasping the kerchief, then to the right. Following this, T'ien Shih reverses her hands towards herself with the right finger in a pointing gesture. Then both hands are held at arms length in front of her, the right hand foremost as T'ien Shih gazes into the distance.

She next turns right and slowly walks to the rear of the stage where she gracefully seats herself on the chair in front of the table. Her left foot protrudes forward slightly beyond the right foot which rests on the toes. Her right hand is placed over the left in her lap and her head is slightly tilted. From this position she first speaks, with her hand gestures accompanying her final lines although her feet remain in the same position. First she holds both hands towards her, right above the left, following this both hands holding the kerchief are moved to the right and then back towards herself with the right hand above the left and the index finger in a pointing gesture. During this pantomime the following words are spoken:

My husband has gone to the mountains to study
As for me, I am so unhappy.
I am T'ien Shih.
My husband is Chuang Tzu.
He has gone to the mountains to study.
I do not see him returning.
I am so unhappy.
So lonely.

After this she rubs the kerchief between both her palms and her hands are moved to the right, then her arms are moved in a circle as though stretching out of weariness. She yawns, placing her right hand to her mouth while holding the kerchief. Her head is inclined right. Then both hands are lowered and she turns to the left on her chair with her left elbow resting on the back of the chair and her head supported on her left hand. He right hand rests on her knee. There is a delicate rotating motion of the body as though in sleep. Suddenly her right leg is crossed over her left and her right hand moved in a wide circular sweep over the right leg. Her legs are again uncrossed and her arms moved front as she shakes her hands, turns left, and swings her hands back to the right. The sequence of movement is then repeated but in the opposite directions.

Next both hands are placed out and brought down to the knees and T'ien Shih proceeds to dust her left arm with the kerchief from the shoulder down and then up again. The left arm then makes a low horizontal sweep to left and then back to the knee in a high arc. Following this T'ien Shih coquettishly extends the left leg and dusts it down, stopping to gaze at it with approval, her kerchief held with both hands to the right of her head which is tilted left. The kerchief is then slowly stretched across her chest with both hands and slowly brought up to cover her face where she catches a corner in her mouth and lowers the kerchief diagonally to reveal her expression of coy amorousness. She releases one end of the kerchief which she playfully flicks away from her and then holds at the right of her face. Now placing both hands on her knees she stands up, left foot to the rear of the right. She walks forward with an anxious air rubbing her kerchief between her palms. Using the same movements, she walks to the left and then to the right, finally returning to stand behind the chair. She places the chair at a slight angle as she gazes to the right and places her kerchief over the back of the chair. She stands with her left foot still to the rear of her right. Then moving her gaze left she gracefully stretches up her right hand as though removing a hairpin from the back of her coiffure. She coyly picks her teeth with the pin as she gazes left. Suddenly she grimaces as she makes a pantomime of pricking herself with the pin. All this is performed in pure mime. T'ien Shih now walks to the front once more rubbing her kerchief between the palms, then she walks to the right and then to the left front.

Crossing the legs, violent movement of any kind, smiling, displays of emotion through facial expression, and, of course, picking the teeth with a hairpin would all have been counted as highly indecorous in the old style Chinese woman, who in the name of wifely virtue was expected to walk with downcast face, never to show her teeth in smile or to look at anyone directly, and in general to make herself completely self-effacing both through her deportment and appearance. Displays such as T'ien Shih's just described, therefore, represented the height of romantic and even erotic suggestion on the Chinese stage and the audience was in no doubt as to the nature of the stage character who was symbolized through these techniques.

In the final passage of this prelude to the first scene T'ien Shih goes through a sequence of gesture patterns which represent her imagining the blisses of the marriage bed; these are climaxed by her running forward to clasp a husband who turns to nothing in her disappointed embrace. This is carried out in two sequences from right to left and left to right diagonally across stage, and in the last sequence T'ien Shih is rudely awakened from her dream by embracing the servant boy who has suddenly entered from the right to bring her tea on a tray. After the shock of this encounter the following dialogue ensues.

TUNG ERH: Drink some tea, mistress.

T'IEN SHIH: I don't want any.

TUNG ERH *(coaxingly):* Oh, just a little.

T'IEN SHIH *(pettishly):* I don't want any.

TUNG ERH *(placatory):* All right, all right, don't have any then. *(Knowingly)* Is Mistress thinking of her husband?

T'IEN SHIH *(enquiringly):* And you?

TUNG ERH *(suggestively):* Oh yes, I'm thinking of him too.

At this point the servant grins at the audience and makes a gesture to suggest the obvious thoughts of his mistress as he disappears, usually amidst laughter for the clowning of the good ch'ou adds its own quality to even the most unsubtle points. When the servant has disappeared T'ien Shih walks slowly towards the right downstage and begins to wind her kerchief round her right index finger with an amatory expression and flicks the loose end of the kerchief outwards in a flirtatious manner. Then turning towards the rear stage she places both hands behind her with the kerchief dangling and starting with small steps she increases speed in a serpentine course which finally carries her off stage through the exit at the rear.

Scene 1: Returning Home

Chuang Tzu enters from the backstage, i.e., to the audience's left. He holds a ying-ch'en, or fly switch in his right hand. He swings this in a circular sweep upwards from the right and downwards to the left as he walks. His gait is the normal pace of the sheng actor, cheng-pu, as described in the opening of the previous play. He comes to a stop with his left arm swinging up and around to the right, the index and third finger extended; then using the same hand he strokes his beard with a long downward sweep. He moves on to the front stage, swinging the switch with his right hand. He extends his left arm and swings the switch in a complete arc as he arrives front stage. His right hand is raised with the index and third finger extended and the switch hanging vertically suspended from his fourth finger.

CHUANG TZU: Respectfully, I received my teacher's orders to come down from the secluded mountains. After visiting T'ien Shih I shall return. *(He gestures with his right hand horizontally and in an arc.)* A few more steps will bring me to my humble courtyard.
(He swings his right hand in a circular motion to grasp the switch again and walks round a few paces until he returns to the starting point to face the servant boy who has just made his entry at the right rear.)
SERVANT BOY: Welcome, master!
(He goes down on his knees with his hands before his face in salute. The right fist is bent against the open palm of the left hand.)
CHUANG TZU: Ah, here is the boy. *(He turns his left palm outwards and gives a slight nod.)*
Return to the house and tell your mistress that the master has returned.
(The boy rises. Chuang Tzu walks round a few paces and repeats his steps before pausing to step over the threshold of

the entrance to his home. This is a deliberate passage of mime that is typical of Chinese stage practice and is used to symbolize passing into a building from out-of-doors or from one part of a building to another, a useful convention on a stage completely devoid of sets. The action completed Chuang Tzu walks to the rear stage and seats himself on the chair at a slight angle to front stage. The servant who has at first walked to the right follows Chuang Tzu and kneels before his seated master. Chuang Tzu beckons him to rise. T'ien Shih enters at the right backstage stopping and delicately holding her kerchief to her right temple as she looks left.)

SERVANT BOY: Mistress, you are wanted.

T'IEN SHIH: Suddenly I hear the boy calling me. What do you want boy? Why do you call your mistress to the second chamber? *(She walks to the center stage front and stands with both hands extended above the right side of her chest the right hand above the left.)*
He says my husband has returned. *(She faces Chuang Tzu, her hands now similarly placed to the left. She points at the servant and looks back.)*
I'll stand in the second chamber and watch. It is indeed my husband who has returned. *(She circles to the left with both hands pointing, the thumbs against the index fingers. She returns to the servant and moves her kerchief in a circular gesture towards him, then looks back and front again.)* I will tell the boy to wait until I have changed my dress.
(T'ien Shih next performs a dance which is characterized by coquettish movement and facial expression. She commences with moving in a circular floor pattern, taking short quick steps on the toes, swinging both arms while holding the kerchief in her right hand. She backs up and moves diagonally across the stage to the rear right. As she goes she lightly tosses the kerchief in the air and catches it with her left hand as she places her right hand on her hip. One shoulder is moving up and down with coy abandon. She stops at the exit (in reality the right entry) and with her right hand above her head looks seductively back over her shoulder and with a quick hop from one foot to the other, making a roguish kick backwards, she disappears. The servant boy looks after her in wonderment and

then goes through the whole performance in parody of his mistress. Each movement is violently caricatured with a certain amount of extra hip wiggling thrown in for good measure. In the middle of his demonstration he appears to wrench his back, turns an anguished face to the audience and hobbles to the left front stage with a glance at the motionless Chuang Tzu on the way. T'ien Shih now makes her re-entry, she has changed her clothes and wears the formal costume with long sleeves described earlier. The silk water sleeves hang to the floor and she enters adjusting these with graceful jerks to hang in folds from the cuffs as she circles at the front stage, turns, mimes stepping over the threshold, and goes toward Chuang Tzu, followed by the servant who then goes to the right front stage as Chuang Tzu rises and takes a few paces left while swinging the fly switch. When T'ien Shih enters the dialogue begins.)

T'IEN SHIH: I have changed my clothes from head to foot. Now I will go and welcome back my lord and master. *(Arrived before Chuang Tzu she shakes her water sleeves back to reveal her hands which are extended palm foremost towards her husband.)*

You have returned home then, husband?

CHUANG TZU *(swinging the switch over his left arm and back again):* I have returned.

(He sits once more and T'ien Shih makes the gesture of dusting his clothes.)

T'IEN SHIH: But look at your face, husband, there is ice on your beard and you are covered with dust.

(Her right hand strokes his beard downwards as she bends toward him. Chuang Tzu turns away from her with disdainful sweep of his hand.)

T'IEN SHIH *(indignantly standing with her hands on hips):* Is that how you show your regard for me?

CHUANG TZU: Don't be so distasteful.

T'IEN SHIH *(points to him and then to herself and steps forward peevishly.):* Ai, ai. We are no longer boy and girl. Have we so much time together? *(She goes towards him hands extended and flicks her left sleeve into position. The property man now places a chair at the left front stage and T'ien Shih seats herself.)*

Very well, if that's how you feel I will stay far away from you.
But I beg you to avoid the word distasteful.
*(Chuang Tzu rises with the switch hanging over his right arm;
he swings it to the left and goes over to T'ien Shih bending over
her with his left foot extended resting on the heel only, his right
hand held above his stomach and left hand over right.)*

CHUANG TZU: Aiya, my sweet wife.
*(T'ien Shih angrily flicks her left sleeve towards him then re-
adjusts it over the cuff and looks scornfully away to the right.)*

T'IEN SHIH: I'm not sweet. I'm bitter.

CHUANG TZU *(bends over her again, laughs, swings the switch over
his right arm and extends his left towards her):* Aiya. T'ien
Shih. This is —
(The servant boy suddenly appears.)

SERVANT BOY: A-hm-m.
*(Chuang Tzu is by this time behind T'ien Shih's chair to the
left.)*

CHUANG TZU: What do you want boy? *(He makes a threatening gesture with his left hand the third finger of which is bent.)*

SERVANT BOY *(raising both hands and ducking):* Waiting for the
master's orders.

CHUANG TZU *(waves his left arm in a grand sweep towards the boy):*
I have no orders. Go away!

SERVANT BOY *(shaking his head):* I shan't.

CHUANG TZU *(flicks the switch over his extended left arm towards
the boy):* Do you want me to beat you?

SERVANT BOY *(ducking to ward off the threatened blow):* No. I'm off.
But when I've gone you should go down on your knees to the
mistress.
*(Chuang Tzu furious, moves towards the boy from the right
of T'ien Shih's chair, and the boy points to T'ien Shih as he
runs off stage.)*

CHUANG TZU: Get out! *(He goes to the left of T'ien Shih and prepares
to kneel. As he does so the servant dashes back and thrusts a
cushion beneath his master's knee. Chuang Tzu makes a furious
exclamation and aims a blow at the boy who avoids it and
quickly disappears again.)* Since I left home that boy's become
impossible. T'ien Shih this is . . . *(He laughs rather hollowly
and kneels first with a wide sweep of the left arm and the left*

leg equally widely postured.) When your husband wishes to talk with you the boy should know he has to disappear. *(He adjusts his right sleeve over the cuff, his left arm is across his chest.)*

T'IEN SHIH: As his mistress I suppose I am to blame.

CHUANG TZU: Who spoke of blame?

(T'ien Shih rises and bends towards Chuang Tzu, indicating he should stand up, then poses with her right hand at her right temple and her left across her waist holding the kerchief. The property man now removes her chair and places it beside Chuang Tzu's chair backstage center. T'ien Shih beckons to Chuang Tzu.)

T'IEN SHIH: Please sit down, husband.

(Chuang Tzu sits extending his left leg in a broad sweep. His right hand rests on his right thigh supporting the switch which is draped over his right arm. He motions with his left hand that T'ien Shih should sit.)

CHUANG TZU: And you also.

(T'ien Shih sits with her kerchief over her right arm. She raises her hands to the left with extended palms toward her husband.)

T'IEN SHIH: Have you finished your metaphysical studies among the high mountains, husband? *(She gestures towards him with her right hand, the index and third finger extended.)* Why have you returned home?

CHUANG TZU *(moves the switch to his left hand and gestures towards T'ien Shih with his right):* I've come back to see you.

T'IEN SHIH *(raising both hands palms towards him):* Thank you indeed for such a kind thought.

CHUANG TZU *(nods his head):* Please.

T'IEN SHIH *(gestures with her right hand towards the right and then points back at Chuang Tzu):* Did you see anything interesting on your way down from the mountains, husband?

CHUANG TZU: A strange thing happened to me.

T'IEN SHIH *(with both hands raised towards him):* What kind of strange thing?

(Chuang Tzu's right hand is on his knee. The left arm is raised; the switch is held in the right hand and falling over the right arm.)

CHUANG TZU: When I reached the foot of the mountains and was traveling on my way I came to a new grave on which the earth was not yet dry. *(His left hand is extended with the index and second fingers outstretched as pointers.)* By the side sat a young woman dressed in mourning who whisked her paper fan over the mound without pausing. *(His hands are placed on his knees, then raised again.)* I went over and asked her who was buried there and why she was fanning the damp earth. *(He gestures with his left hand, the index and second fingers outstretched. He then places his hands on his knees again.)* The young woman replied that it was her husband who had loved her dearly and on his deathbed he had asked her not to marry again before the earth on his grave was dry. This was the reason for her action she told me and wept piteously. Moved by her tears I took charge. *(He raises his left hand with the thumb and index fingers bent together in a curve and the remaining three fingers outstretched.)* And within three minutes dried the grave through my magic powers. To show her gratitude she presented me with her little fan. *(Chuang Tzu places the switch in his left hand and reaches out with his right hand to take a fan which is on the table and this he gives to T'ien Shih with a wide gesture.)* Please look at it, T'ien Shih.

(T'ien Shih takes the fan, rises and, goes to the center of the front stage where she opens the fan. She stands with her right foot to the rear of her left foot and reads from right to left and top to bottom of the fan.)

T'IEN SHIH: Let me see it. *(Reads.)*

Taoist traveler who pitied me,
When you return home tell your wife
That she would be no more virtuous
Than I have been.

(T'ien Shih frowns deeply as she reads and finally spits on the fan and tears it in two, casting one half on the floor to the right and the other half to the left.)

Aiya. What kind of talk is this. She's just a cheap woman.

CHUANG TZU *(steps towards her, pointing with the index and second finger of his left hand. He stands with left foot extended and flicks his switch with a circular sweep):* T'ien Shih why have you destroyed the fan?

T'IEN SHIH *(gesturing with her right hand):* Because it offends me deeply. *(She faces Chuang Tzu with her right hand held out, palm up, index finger and thumb together and the other fingers bent.)* Oh husband. *(She places her hands on her chest as she speaks.)* How can you compare me to that common person when I belong to the Emperor of Ch'i's family?

CHUANG TZU: Aiya! You belong to the Emperor of Ch'i's family, how could I compare you to that common person. It is difficult to fathom people's minds today that's all. *(He points towards her with the index and second finger of his left hand which he then brings round in a sweep from the shoulder.)*

T'IEN SHIH: Whatever happens to you I shall be faithful. *(She gestures towards him with both hands, palms outwards, left hand slightly higher than the right.)*

CHUANG TZU: You cannot.

T'IEN SHIH: Certainly I can.

CHUANG TZU: I don't believe it.

T'IEN SHIH: I swear it before heaven. *(She faces front with her hands lifted as high as her head, palms together.)*

CHUANG TZU: All right, swear. Then I can be easy in my mind. *(He extends his right arm, index and second fingers as pointers.)*

T'IEN SHIH: Ah, my husband. We sit together, my husband. *(She extends her arms towards him. Chuang Tzu makes a gesture of restraint with his left hand.)* My husband. *(She steps towards him and strokes his beard with her right hand.)*

CHUANG TZU: Holiest Buddha. *(His left arm is held bent in front of his body, palm outward as though in blessing, his right arm is across his waist.)*

T'IEN SHIH: Alas. *(She stands back a little, right foot behind left and the left arm held up and supported under the elbow by the right fingers.)* Listen carefully to your wife's words. *(She points at him with both hands whose index fingers touch the centers of the thumbs.)* Even though you die first. I shall always remain constant and true. If I should falter . . . show any indecision . . . *(She steps forward and kneels facing front stage, her left hand*

is raised with the index finger and thumb together. Chuang Tzu
takes a step forward, his hand raised towards her.)

CHUANG TZU: Well?

T'IEN SHIH: I shall prepare for heaven to strike me down. *(She*
swings her hands toward him, the left pointing directly at him
and the right pointing under left elbow.)

CHUANG TZU: How? *(Both hands gesture to the left.)*

T'IEN SHIH: With five blasts of thunder and lightning.

CHUANG TZU: Ah-ah. Even though T'ien Shih has sworn an oath
I am not convinced in my own mind. I'll ask her to go and
prepare some tea for the moment.

(His hands gesture to the left, the thumb and second finger
of the left hand are joined. He then strokes his beard with the
left hand. He motions T'ien Shih to rise with a sweeping ges-
ture. T'ien Shih rises pointing left, then right, as she does so
before adjusting her sleeves.)

T'IEN SHIH: I shall not be long. I'll go and make some tea. *(She faces*
right and exits right rear stage with her left hand held behind
and the water sleeve wrapped round it.)

CHUANG TZU: There she goes and while she is away I can reflect in
secret. *(He has turned and gone center front stage watching*
T'ien Shih go. His right arm holding the switch is extended. He
turns to face front with the index and second fingers of his right
hand extended, leaving the switch hanging loosely down. He
then makes a short turn left and grasps the switch again.)

Now let me see. I can tell by her every glance that she has
no intention of remaining a widow. I know. I'll pretend to die
and then we'll see how T'ien Shih keeps her resolution. I'll sit
beyond in the second chamber and wait for T'ien Shih to return. Then I shall see what happens.

(He mimes crossing the threshold, and swinging the switch
in broad circles he goes with wide steps to the chair behind the
table at the rear of the stage. There he flings the switch on the
table and sits, hands on knees. T'ien Shih enters backstage
right carrying a tray with a teacup in her left hand which she
holds shoulder height. He right arm is held across her body
to the left. She comes to front stage right, walking a serpentine
course to get there. She flings the right sleeve at full length and
then readjusts it over the cuff before turning and going to the

right of the table where she puts down the teacup before Chuang Tzu.)

T'IEN SHIH: I hurry to the second chamber to take my husband some tea.

(Chuang Tzu takes up the cup and drinks. He holds the cup with his right hand to his mouth while the left hand with extended fingers is placed before the right hand. In this position the head is tilted backwards as though drinking, the hands in the same position throughout the action. T'ien Shih stands facing front while he drinks. Her right arm is across her waist and her left arm bent at the elbow is held above. When Chuang Tzu has drained his cup he puts it down and immediately clutches his stomach with both hands, his face expressing agony. The right hand is above the left.)

CHUANG TZU: Having taken the tea I shout loudly as though in grievous pain and clutch my stomach.

(T'ien Shih agitatedly cries out.)

T'IEN SHIH: Whatever is the matter?

(She runs around the table to left back stage and summons the servant boy and then returns to her original position. The servant boy rushes on, going round in circles, returning to the right of the table, looking perplexedly first at his master, then the audience and shaking his upturned hands, an action also performed by T'ien Shih. The boy finally goes to the left of Chuang Tzu. Chuang Tzu swings his head sharply right and then sharply left, his beard emphasizing this pendulum-like motion also accented by T'ien Shih and the servant boy who move towards Chuang Tzu each time he swings away. As he swings towards T'ien Shih she cries "Husband" and as he swings towards the servant the latter cries "Master.")

CHUANG TZU: Probably life is ended for me. It is the third watch and the King of Hades has decreed I die today. Who can save me before the fifth watch? T'ien Shih! Boy!

(Chuang Tzu slumps over the table with his outstretched water sleeves hanging down over the table. He is shaking his head violently, he crosses his eyes, half rises in his seat and then falls limply back in it, head inclined right. T'ien Shih swings round, flinging out her sleeves in agitation. She kneels first on the right knee and then on both and flings her sleeves behind her before

adjusting them to hang over her cuffs. The servant boy is kneeling at Chuang Tzu's left helplessly shaking his hands.)

T'IEN SHIH: No sooner has my husband returned than I must mourn him.

(Chuang Tzu stands up and walks to the front center stage, making broad sweeps with the switch. He pauses and flicks the switch over his right shoulder.)

CHUANG TZU: I'll see what you decide to do now.

(He turns, mimes crossing the threshold, and strides off at the rear left. T'ien Shih stands up and goes to center stage with her hands crossed across her heart.)

T'IEN SHIH: How can I express the grief in my heart. *(She turns left and walks back up the center towards the table where she and the servant boy carry out an imaginary corpse.)*

I must bury Chuang Tzu's corpse quickly. I'll call the boy and give him his instructions. *(She and the servant boy return to the front center stage. T'ien Shih beckons the servant boy, her right hand holding the left sleeve as she does so.)*

Boy, your master is dead. Here are fifty ounces of silver. *(She returns to the table and then back to the boy as though carrying the silver.)* Take it and go out into the town and bargain for a reasonably good coffin. *(She indicates the coffin by spreading out her arms and then moving them downwards slightly.)* Buy a paper boy effigy,[1] also a girl. Get gold paper money and silver as well. Be off quickly.

(She points at the boy and weeping circles the stage and goes off. The boy follows her, howling loudly, and the curtain is drawn.)

Scene 2

Immediately the servant boy appears in front of it and addresses the audience from the center. (The use of a curtain was un-

---

1. It was the Chinese belief that the soul of a dead person traveled to the underworld and passed the time before reincarnation in the city ruled by Yama, lord of the underworld. With a view to providing for this existence in the next world, various earthly needs such as servants, money, sedan chairs, and so on were reproduced in paper and then burned at a funeral in the belief that the articles so treated would serve the needs of the deceased person.

known in the old style traditional Chinese theater but in this play it serves a technical need by allowing the elaborate tableau required in the next scene to be arranged without spoiling the effect for the audience.)

SERVANT BOY *(hand outstretched to audience):* Aiya. What do you think of that? *(Leaning backward.)* Our master had just returned home, hadn't even had a meal, only sipped a cup of tea and he died. Just like that! Now the mistress has asked me to buy a coffin. I wonder where's the best place to get one? *(He scratches his head perplexedly.)* Well, I'll go and have a look around.
(He circles the stage area front left, shielding his eyes.) Ah! Here we are. *(He goes downstage right and mimes stepping over the threshold.)* Wait, I'll just hop inside. *(He addresses audience and then calls to an invisible shopkeeper behind the curtain, waving his right hand as he bawls.)* Hi! Shopkeeper!

VOICE BEHIND CURTAIN *(sepulchrally):* What do you want?

SERVANT BOY: To buy a coffin.

VOICE BEHIND CURTAIN: How many do you want?

SERVANT BOY *(turns to audience with a resigned shrug):* How many do you usually need for one dead man?

VOICE BEHIND CURTAIN *(in same sepulchral tone):* Which one would you like?

SERVANT BOY: Wait until I have a look round. *(He walks round inspecting invisible coffins.)* Ah, this one's not bad. How much is it?

VOICE BEHIND CURTAIN: Fifty pieces of silver.

SERVANT BOY *(turns his head, expressing comic dismay, and scratches his head with his right hand as he surveys the audience):* What! So expensive? I'll give you twenty pieces.

VOICE BEHIND CURTAIN: Twenty's too low, make it more.

SERVANT BOY *(holds out his index and second fingers, the thumb holding down the other two fingers, as he gestures while bargaining):* Twenty-five pieces then.

VOICE BEHIND CURTAIN: Can't possibly sell at that price.

SERVANT BOY *(he now extends his first three fingers):* Can't sell at twenty five? Well, what about thirty?

VOICE BEHIND CURTAIN: It's a deal.

SERVANT BOY: I knew you'd come down a bit. Wait until I take it away — *(He circles round the stage area.)*

VOICE BEHIND CURTAIN: Hurry up then.

SERVANT BOY: I want to buy a paper boy effigy and a girl also. Wait, I'll be back. *(He goes off front stage right and comes back downstage right.)* Well, here I am at the shop counter.

VOICE BEHIND CURTAIN *(it is the same voice):* What do you want?

SERVANT BOY: I want to buy a boy effigy, also a girl. *(He looks at the audience perplexedly, pointing with his thumb to indicate astonishment at hearing the same shopkeeper again.)*

VOICE BEHIND CURTAIN: We've no girls, only boys.

SERVANT BOY *(placing his hands behind him on his buttocks):* Only boys, eh? Well, how much do you want for one?

VOICE BEHIND CURTAIN: Four hundred large coppers.

SERVANT BOY *(showing his dismay to audience and then turning to hold up his left index finger):* Give you one hundred.

VOICE BEHIND CURTAIN: Nothing doing.

SERVANT BOY *(holds up index finger, then all five fingers):* One hundred and fifty then.

VOICE BEHIND CURTAIN: Nothing doing.

SERVANT BOY *(holding up index and second fingers):* Two hundred then.

VOICE BEHIND CURTAIN: Nothing doing.

SERVANT BOY *(holding up two fingers and then all five, palm outwards):* Two hundred and fifty then.[2] How about that?

VOICE BEHIND CURTAIN *(without changing tone):* Sold.

SERVANT BOY: Leave it here while I go off to buy a girl effigy. *(He walks round to find an imaginary shop counter center stage.)*

VOICE BEHIND CURTAIN *(the same voice again):* What do you want? *(Servant expresses his astonishment to audience.)*

SERVANT BOY: Do you happen to have any boy or girl effigies for sale?

VOICE BEHIND CURTAIN: We've only got girls, no boys.

SERVANT BOY: Ah, just what I want. I'll take one of your girls. How much are they?

2. "Two hundred and fifty," *erh-pai wu*, was a nickname for a fool. It was a reference to the fact that 250 copper cash was an impossible monetary sum in old Peking where five copper cash were reckoned as being a unit of twenty.

VOICE BEHIND CURTAIN: Three hundred large coppers. *(The servant boy grimaces to audience at the high price.)*

SERVANT BOY *(indicates one hundred and fifty with his fingers):* Give you one hundred and fifty.

VOICE BEHIND CURTAIN: Nothing doing.

SERVANT BOY: Two hundred then. *(He holds up his index and second fingers.)*

VOICE BEHIND CURTAIN: It's yours.

SERVANT BOY: Wait until I call a porter. Hi. Take this coffin and carry it away. I'll take the paper effigies on my back. Ah, the coffin's arrived. There. Everything's arranged. Now I'll call the mistress.

(Showing satisfaction, he steps over the threshold and then suddenly remembering he is in mourning, begins to wail. He circles the stage and exits rear left still wailing.)

(The curtain is now drawn to reveal the mourning chamber. A coffin stands on a trestle at the left rear. A boy effigy stands on a chair at the left of the coffin. He holds a long pipe in one hand, a taper in the other, and a tobacco pouch dangles from the pipe. His arms are bent at the elbows and he leans forward. A girl effigy stands upright on a chair at the right of the coffin and holds a tray in both hands. The eyes of both figures are closed and they are absolutely immobile. Two lighted candles, an incense holder, and a wooden name tablet stand before the coffin. The servant boy enters from the right, he is dressed in a white gown and carries a white switch representing a feather duster in his hand. He mimes stepping over the threshold, circles the stage completely, and then goes down on his knees before the coffin, touching the floor with his forehead four times and raising his right foot high behind him each time in parody of an obeisance. He then rises, goes to the coffin, dusts it with his switch, and then he goes left stage to call his mistress.)

T'IEN SHIH *(off stage):* My husband.

(She enters from upstage left dressed in the white mourning dress described in the section on costume. She is weeping with her right hand held gracefully before her eyes. She circles the stage once after miming stepping over the threshold. She pauses right foot behind left, then goes to the coffin, takes an incense

taper, turns around and returns to the coffin. She then returns front with both hands held at either side to her temples. She flings her sleeves out and adjusts them before going down on her knees before the coffin and making an obeisance three times. The servant imitates her. She then stands and cries three times)

Husband, husband, husband *(stamping her foot on the last word and holding her left hand to her eyes. She comes to the front of the stage and kneels before the audience.)*
This T'ien Shih goes down on her knees. Listen to your wife's words. *(Her hands are held in front of her with the index fingers and thumbs together and the right hand in front of the left.)* Today you have died and so all is ended. Left alone, who am I to lean on now? *(She moves her right hand out in a circular sweep and then back to herself.)* Who can I turn to for help? I must rise and give the boy his orders.

(She rises and calls the boy, extending her right hand.) Boy. You wait here and if anyone calls to offer condolences come and let me know.

(She gestures towards herself and then the boy. Her hands are next brought to her chest and the right hand extended after this. Then both hands gesture toward the boy. Finally placing her right hand before her eyes she begins weeping loudly again and makes a serpentine course towards the exit at the left.)

SERVANT BOY: All right.

(To audience.) You see, the mistress wants me to wait here in case anyone calls.

(He begins to wail and walks up and down. Then stops, looks at the paper boy effigy, glances mischievously at the audience and gently touches the paper boy with his switch. The effigy sways lightly backwards and forwards to the servant boy's glee. He then blows at the paper boy who rocks gently once more and the servant cries his delight to the audience. Then he looks at the incense burning before the coffin and seizing a taper, he looks knowingly at the audience, places it near his nose and gives a tremendous sneeze. He is just about to hold it to the paper boy's nose when a loud voice is heard off stage. He gives a start.)

CHUANG TZU *(off stage):* Holiest Buddha!

SERVANT BOY: Oh. Somebody's coming. I must be off.
(He mimes stepping over the threshold and quickly runs off stage at the left. Chuang Tzu strides on at the right. He wears the elaborate pa-kua robe described earlier and in his left hand he carries a long staff with an ornately carved dragon's head at the top and silk tassels dangling from the staff. The fly switch hangs from the third finger of his right hand and his closed fan is inserted in the collar of his robe at the back of his right shoulder, a typical stage convention when the actor's hands are otherwise engaged. He comes to the front stage and extends his right hand, index and second finger extended with the switch hanging down from the third finger to which it is looped. His left foot rests on the heel with toe of the boot raised.)

CHUANG TZU: I raise the dragon head staff. I need no human aid. *(He places his left foot on the ground again.)* With these few words I strike fear into men's hearts. *(He moves his right hand slowly left and then right and finally swings it over in a wide arc across his body, the palm downwards.)*
When we are alive we are promised love everlasting but dead we are given only a fan to dry the grave. It is easier to dispose of the tiger's skin than his bones. *(He makes a circular gesture with his open palm against his beard.)* We can know men's faces but not their hearts. *(He gestures towards his heart.)* I am dead, really dead. I am dead. I am the Taoist of the southern seas. I am also Chuang Tzu who pretended to die in the second chamber. *(He grasps the fly switch in his right hand, holds it out to the right and flicks it over his left arm as he inclines his body forward. Then he swings it out with a sweep to the right.)*
Now will T'ien Shih keep her resolution to remain faithful? I will go into the mourning chamber and find out. *(He mimes stepping over the threshold, walks towards the coffin, and surveys the mourning arrangements.)*
Hm. The funeral arrangements are all very proper. Here is gold paper money and silver, a paper boy effigy and also a girl.
(He faces the effigies, grasping his fly switch which he lets drop to hang by the thong as he points with index and second finger of the right hand.) We can ignore the girl but the boy looks exactly as though he were alive. *(He gestures with his right hand, palm outwards, walks towards backstage, and stands to face*

obliquely front towards the boy effigy. He raises his hand to point with his index and second finger.)

Ah, paper boy, your master will turn you into a real person; I will trace out your birthdays with the eight magic symbols and transform you into a man who can talk. *(He walks a few steps forward, faces front, makes a circular gesture against his beard and transfers the fly switch to the fingers of his left hand. He then takes the fan from his collar and flicks it open to the right.)*
At the first wave of my fan you will turn your head. *(He moves the fan up and down to the rapid beat of a gong. He steps back a few paces and holding the open fan horizontally he waves it slowly upward with the paper boy's head moving in time to the fan and the precise beat of the gong. Then reversing his wrist so that his palm faces downwards he brings the paper boy's head downwards in time to his fan movement.)*
At the second you will open your eyes. *(A swift flick of the fan and the paper boy's eyes open.)*
At the third wave you will move your hands. *(He waves his fan up and down with one swift movement and the paper boy drops his hands to his sides. The property man who has been waiting for this moment relieves the paper boy of his pipe and taper.)*
And at the fourth wave you will follow your master.
(Chuang Tzu now waves his fan in quick short movements towards the right and left. He stands with his legs apart. The paper boy moves in time to his fan. Chuang Tzu takes a few steps towards the paper boy and makes him slowly lift his left arm in time to the fan, followed by his right arm, his right leg and his left leg in turn. It is all done with hair breadth precision and requires the most skillful mime on the part of the actor playing the paper boy. Finally Chuang waves his puppet off the chair and the paper boy stiffly raises his left leg, jumps down, and walking stiffly with broad strides and rigidly outstretched arms he takes four paces across the stage, turns squarely on the fifth, and takes two paces to the front. He is followed by Chuang Tzu.)
Wait. Now you are just like a real person. Open your mouth. *(He waves his right hand. The paper boy opens his mouth like a gaping fish but no sound emerges.)* Make a greeting. *(The*

paper boy places his hands stiffly together and pumps them up and down before his chest.) Speak. *(Again the paper boy's mouth is like a cave but there is no sound as he moves his lips helplessly.)* But wait a minute. It will be difficult to speak without a tongue. Ah, looking around I see a small bird fluttering around the eaves. I take my fan and catch him and here's his tongue for you. *(Chuang Tzu mimes catching the bird with his hand, reaches out as though to grasp the bird, and throws it at the paper boy who is standing woodenly waiting.)* Now. Speak.

PAPER BOY *(slowly opens his mouth and repeats the word after Chuang Tzu in a squeaky treble):* Speak.

CHUNG TZU: This.

PAPER BOY *(in the same faltering squeak):* This.

CHUANG TZU: Ho, ho, ho.

(The paper boy laughs rapidly and shuts his mouth like a trap.)

PAPER BOY: Ho, ho, ho.

CHUANG TZU *(he opens his fan backs away a step and turns with a satisfied look at the paper boy):* Now the paper boy can speak. Go into the mourning chamber and call the servant boy. Your master gives you a clear order. *(He waves the paper boy away. The latter turns sharply and strides off with the stiff jerky gait of a puppet.)* The paper boy has gone out but wait a minute the girl is still here. When T'ien Shih returns she will certainly ask where the paper boy went. I'll make a magic fire to burn her up and when T'ien Shih comes back she won't notice so quickly that the paper boy has gone. *(He closes his fan and points at the girl effigy with the index and second fingers of his right hand. He holds the closed fan at right angles in his hand, circles the stage and goes back to face the girl effigy who still stands motionless on the chair. He then opens his fan with a flourish and waves it at the girl who jumps down and runs off stage quickly.)* Now the girl is burnt up by magic fire and suddenly an idea comes to mind. *(He closes his fan and holds it first to the left and then to the right.)* I'll turn myself into a handsome young gentleman who has come to offer his condolences. *(He circles his fan in space.)* Then we shall see how T'ien Shih behaves. *(He opens his fan held at the horizontal, turns towards the rear stage, and strides off towards the left exit with the fan held high in his right hand and his left arm extended.)* In this way I can know her true feelings.

(As Chuang Tzu exits the hua-shen or spirit representing the handsome young man into whom Chuang Tzu has transformed himself makes his entry at the right. He wears the costume described earlier and holds his fan in front of his face, shaking it with a trembling motion of the wrist. He stops center front stage and closes the fan with his left hand after lowering it gradually and emphasizing this final gesture with a nod of his head. He stands resting his left foot on the heel. He then walks round left and faces center. The paper boy enters at this point and they both circle the stage together. The spirit comes to a halt left stage with the paper boy at center stage. The spirit then goes to right stage. His closed fan is held in his right hand against the center of his body which tilts forward slightly. The property man brings a chair on which the spirit seats himself with a flourish of his fan as he opens it in his right hand and brings it to his chest. His left foot rests on the heel and his chair is placed obliquely to face center stage.)

THE SPIRIT: I'll tell the boy once more how he must behave and what he must do. Boy. First of all, go and knock on the door and say that a young prince from Ch'u-kuo has come to pay his respects and offer condolences.

PAPER BOY *(standing stiffly facing front):* I understand. There's somebody rumbling about inside.

(At this moment the servant boy enters at left stage yawning and stretching.)

SERVANT BOY: Whoever can this be, screeching and kicking up such a din?

(With a start he comes face to face with the paper boy. He gestures in confusion right and left, looking first to the chair where the paper boy formerly stood and then back to the paper boy himself. The servant boy now sets off in a counter-clockwise direction as though running furiously, elbows up and head down. Actually he takes very short steps and runs in small

circles. The paper boy now quickly hops up on his chair again; the property man hands him his pipe and taper and it is as though he had never been brought to life. The servant boy draws up with a start opposite the paper boy and gazes in astonishment first at the effigy, then at the audience. He now sets off running in the opposite direction, and the paper boy quickly hops down and returns to center stage where the defeated servant boy comes face to face with him once more. The whole pantomime is repeated in sequence until the servant boy faces the paper boy center stage again.)

SERVANT BOY: What? Why, it's the paper boy I bought for two hundred and fifty big coppers a little while ago. How's he come to be alive? Hello, "Two hundred and fifty."

PAPER BOY: Why do you call me "Two hundred and fifty"?

SERVANT BOY: Don't you know? Well, the master died and I paid two hundred and fifty big coppers for an effigy just like you. That's why I call you by that name.

PAPER BOY *(haughtily):* The one you bought was made of paper but I'm a real person.

SERVANT BOY: Oh, I see. All right, well, I won't call you that then.

PAPER BOY: We are mourners come to pay our respects.

SERVANT BOY *(abruptly):* Wait here. Mistress, some mourners have arrived.

(T'ien Shih enters and goes to sit on a chair placed by the property man at the left side of the coffin. She sits holding the bottom of her left water sleeve with her right hand.)

T'IEN SHIH: Ask them who they are.

SERVANT BOY: Right, I'll go and ask them. Hey. "Two hundred and fifty!"

(The servant boy calls from center stage. The paper boy is over against the seated spirit who of course has not left the stage all this time. The paper boy walks stiffly over to the servant boy.)

PAPER BOY: Why do you call me by that name again?

SERVANT BOY *(he skips towards the paper boy, holding up his right hand):* Sorry, my mistake. Where are you people from?

PAPER BOY *(extends his right hand, turns and points to the spirit and then turns back to the servant boy with his head held high and a haughty mien):* It's a young prince of Ch'u-kuo who has come to pay his respects.

SERVANT BOY: I see. I'll go and tell the mistress.

The paper boy strides towards the servant, makes a sharp turn about and nearly kicks the servant from the rear before walking back to right stage. The servant boy makes an angry gesture before calling to his mistress as he goes back to her.)

It's a young prince from Ch'u-kuo.

T'IEN SHIH *(remaining seated and pointing with her left hand):* Go out and deliver this message. *(She extends both hands to the right.)* Say your mistress is in mourning. *(Her hands move to the left and swing out in an arc, palms upward.)* And cannot go out to receive him. *(Her hands are placed to left waist, left palm up and right hand over it.)*

But tell him to come in himself.

SERVANT BOY *(looks at T'ien Shih dubiously):* Right. Well, that's a new one. Here, "Two hundred and fifty!"

(He calls brusquely from center stage. The paper boy strides stiffly forward as though he is going to trample the servant who quickly leaps back a pace or two to the left. The paper boy turns sharply and returns center, followed by the servant.)

PAPER BOY: Did you call?

SERVANT BOY *(angrily):* I certainly did.

PAPER BOY: What about? *(He stands stiffly before the servant.)*

SERVANT BOY: The mistress is in mourning and can't come out herself to receive you. But I presume the young gentleman's not a stranger as he's invited to come inside himself.

(The servant has turned away from the paper boy as he talks and holds his head contemptuously as he extends his right arm upwards. The paper boy pretends to snap at his nose and returns to his master to whom he stiffly extends his left arm and inclines his body. The servant waits indignantly at left front stage.)

PAPER BOY: They say you can go in yourself.

(The spirit stands opening his fan, then closes it. He faces rear then mimes stepping over the threshold, left foot raised first. He makes a complete turn round towards the coffin and kneels by going down on his right knee, his arms bent from the elbows, palms together.)

THE SPIRIT: Ha, ha. Then let us go into the mourning chamber and kneel down so that my dead teacher may hear my prayers. In dying he has left his disciple without a guide.

(T'ien Shih stands and goes to front stage, left hand across her waist touching her right sleeve. She kneels at the same time as the spirit, her right hand held to her right temple, left arm across her chest. Then she returns to her chair as the spirit rises and returns to his former seat where he sits with a flourish of his left sleeve to accompany his action. T'ien Shih rises and goes center front, right sleeve concealing her face from the spirit and lightly held with her left hand as she coyly peeps at him.)

T'IEN SHIH: But what do I see before me? A most handsome young man. *(Both her hands are placed right.)* What looks! *(She circles left hand towards him.)*

I would gladly take him for a husband. *(Her right hand is at right temple. She backs up stage left a little.)*

How can I curb my impatience and how shall this slave let him know her desire. *(She holds both hands to the right, thumbs and index fingers together, palms down. She then takes a few steps towards the spirit again.)*

SERVANT BOY *(looks in dismay and thrusts his right knuckle in his eye and sets up a wail):* Aiya! My master.

T'IEN SHIH *(flinging her arm angrily towards the servant):* How the boy weeps.

(She retires to her seat, holding her mourning veil with her left hand to the rear. She adjusts both sleeves over their cuffs as she sits. The spirit stands up, extending his left hand towards the paper boy.)

THE SPIRIT: Boy, go and tell them that having paid our respects we are now departing.

(The paper boy contemptuously calls the servant boy center stage.)

PAPER BOY: Little son, we are leaving. *(He flings out his left hand, kicks back his left foot, and turns sharply back to the right front stage.)*

SERVANT BOY *(with a disgusted shrug):* They're going, mistress. Have you any message?

T'IEN SHIH *(extends right hand towards him, pointing with index and third fingers, then gestures with both hands towards herself):* Boy, go out and tell them to wait. I have a riddle to ask.

If they guess it they may leave; if they cannot I will not let them go. *(She extends both index fingers in pointing gesture with the third finger and thumb placed together.)*

SERVANT BOY *(not moving):* Why do you want to keep them here?

T'IEN SHIH *(stands and goes towards servant, raising her left hand sharply towards him and then back at herself):* Are you going or not?

SERVANT BOY *(doggedly):* I'm not!

T'IEN SHIH: Then I shall have to beat you! *(She raises her left hand at him, holding the bottom of her left sleeve with right hand placed across her chest.)*

SERVANT BOY *(flinching):* All right, I'll go.

T'IEN SHIH *(waving her hand and seating herself again):* Well, hurry up then!

SERVANT BOY *(returning center stage and calling the paper boy):* All right, all right. Hey, "Two hundred and fifty." *(The paper boy walks quickly towards him but does not stop and the servant boy is nearly pushed off the stage until he cries)* Stop! *(The paper boy turns sharply and returns to the center. The servant boy follows him, faces front and extends his right hand.)* The mistress told me to call you back. She has a riddle to ask. If you can guess it you can go; otherwise you can't! *(The paper boy returns to the spirit.)*

PAPER BOY: She has a riddle; if we don't guess it she won't let us leave.

THE SPIRIT: What riddle?

PAPER BOY *(returns center stage):* What riddle?

SERVANT BOY *(faces front and holds both hands down with a completely helpless air):* I don't know either. Mistress, what riddle?

T'IEN SHIH: All lovers know that *(Her right hand is placed against her temple and then back to her waist.)* Youth passes with the years. *(She points forward with index and third finger of right hand extended.)* Is it not better to loosen the jade buckle together *(She gently waves her hand left.)* Before growing old? *(She crosses the index fingers of both hands before replacing them in position on her waist.)*

SERVANT BOY *(gesturing in exasperation at her left):* Well, what are you trying to say. Tell me the whole of it now and save me so much running backwards and forwards.

T'IEN SHIH *(extending her arm, palm outwards, towards him):* That's
   all.
SERVANT BOY: All right . . . if you say so.
PAPER BOY *(returning to center stage):* What's the riddle?
SERVANT BOY: All lovers . . .
PAPER BOY *(quickly and looking straight to the front):* . . . know
   . . .
SERVANT BOY: That youth passes with the . . .
PAPER BOY *(inclining his head indifferently to the right):* . . . years
   . . .
SERVANT BOY: Is it not better to loosen the jade buckle . . .
PAPER BOY *(both hands stiffly by his sides and facing front):* . . .
   together . . .
SERVANT BOY *(to the audience in disgust):* How does he know it all?
   (Extending right hand and talking quickly to paper boy): Well,
   you don't know this bit.
   Before growing . . .
PAPER BOY *(snapping the word out):* . . . old?
SERVANT BOY *(dismayed):* Aiya! How do you know all that?
PAPER BOY: Just a minute! *(He turns sharply to the servant boy who
   goes to the front stage left; then the paper boy speaks to the
   spirit standing to the left of his chair.)*
   All lovers know that
   Youth passes with the years.
   Is it not better to loosen the jade buckle together
   Before growing old?
THE SPIRIT: Go and tell her that I understand the meaning of the
   riddle. But first of all she must obey three important conditions.
   *(He puts out his right hand and, placing the index finger and
   the thumb together, indicates the number with the remaining
   three fingers.)*
PAPER BOY *(repeating the spirit's gestures as he relays the informa-
   tion to the servant boy):* Right. There are three important con-
   ditions to obey.
   *(The servant boy relays the information to T'ien Shih, extend-
   ing his right hand.)*
SERVANT BOY: Mistress, there are three important conditions you
   must obey.
T'IEN SHIH *(raising her right hand towards him):* What are they?
SERVANT BOY: I didn't ask.

T'IEN SHIH (*impatiently pointing with index finger of right hand, thumb and third finger together, left hand holding right sleeve*): Then go and do so. (*She then raises her left hand at him.*)

SERVANT BOY: If I don't go I'll be beaten, I suppose. "Two hundred and fifty," what are the conditions?

(*The paper boy turns to the spirit to wait for the conditions.*)

THE SPIRIT: The first is to throw away the memorial tablet inscribed with your husband's name. (*The spirit sits with legs apart, his closed fan held against his body.*)

The second is to change your mourning for a bridal dress, and the third is to carry out the wedding ceremonies immediately. (*He extends his left arm.*)

PAPER BOY (*goes center stage and repeats the spirit's words to the servant boy, imitating the final gesture at the end*): The first condition is that you must throw away the memorial tablet inscribed with your master's name.

SERVANT BOY: Oh, go and let off wind.

PAPER BOY: The second is to change your mourning for a bridal dress.

SERVANT BOY: What? And she's not yet out of her official period of mourning.

PAPER BOY: And the third condition is to get married immediately.

SERVANT BOY: And let off wind again.

(*The paper boy turns sharply and goes to the right front. Servant turns to his mistress.*)

Mistress, the first condition is that you must throw away the memorial tablet inscribed with the master's name.

T'IEN SHIH: What did you say? Throw away the master's memorial tablet?

SERVANT BOY: It's impossible.

(*T'ien Shih lifts the tablet from the table with her right hand. She transfers it to her left hand, placing her right hand to her eyes as she weeps. She peeps over her sleeve at the handsome young prince. She smiles with delight and deliberately flings the tablet to the floor.*)

Master, ah — ah — (*He sobs loudly.*)

T'IEN SHIH (*stands up angrily and flicks her right sleeve at him.*): What are you weeping about?

SERVANT BOY: You ordered me to throw away my master's memorial tablet, why shouldn't I weep?

T'IEN SHIH *(returning to her seat):* Because I don't want you to weep. And the second condition? *(She holds up her hand.)*

SERVANT BOY: He told me to say that you must change your mourning for a bridal dress.

T'IEN SHIH: Well, that's natural enough. And the third condition?

SERVANT BOY: It should please you. To get married immediately.

(Each time that T'ien Shih asks the conditions the servant boy goes center stage to the paper boy who returns to the spirit. After answering the second condition the paper boy cocks a snook at the exasperated boy, and after the third the paper boy jumps in the air with a scissors-like kick of his legs at the boy before turning to return to the front stage right. There is a constant coming and going between the two clowns during this period of question and answer which ends with a full display of contempt by the paper boy and a climax of frustrated anger on the part of the servant.)

T'IEN SHIH: Go outside and say that we'll comply with the conditions. Invite the gentleman into the study to change his clothes. *(She gestures with her left hand towards the left, then both hands to the right, the left hand supporting the right elbow. She then returns to her seat with her right hand behind her as she walks.)*

SERVANT BOY: Very well. *(He goes disgustedly towards the paper boy.)* "Two hundred and fifty," tell the gentleman to step into the study and change his clothes. *(The paper boy returns to the spirit who stands, gives a knowing look, and closes his fan sharply. He gestures with both hands to the left, turns right and paces the right extreme of the stage to make his exit, stiffly followed by the paper boy.)*

T'IEN SHIH *(stands):* Boy, follow me and change your clothes. *(She flicks her right sleeve at him, points at him, and then brings both hands back to indicate herself.)*

SERVANT BOY: I've no need to.

T'IEN SHIH: Wait while I get ready for the wedding ceremony. *(She flicks both sleeves downwards, then flings the right over the left.*

Makes a circle with her left hand held high and exits along a serpentine course with her right hand behind her back.)

SERVANT BOY *(bursting into tears):* Ah, master, master.

(He has his knuckles to his eyes and makes a derogatory gesture at his retreating mistress as he follows her off stage. He enters again wailing and goes to bang on the table holding the coffin with his switch. He puts his left hand on his head, right hand held in front with five fingers down, making a derogatory gesture indicating the lowest summing up of his mistress's affairs. Then he walks backwards and forwards in a distraught way, weeping and banging on the coffin with his switch.

The spirit enters right backstage and pauses, right foot resting on his heel, his closed fan in his right hand. He goes to center stage, flicks open his fan and turns to face the rear stage as T'ien Shih appears. Both have changed into their richly brocaded bridal clothes. T'ien Shih stops and lifts both hands to the left temple and then to the right. They both walk together to front stage. They kneel. T'ien Shih is on both knees, right arm across her waist, both arms held delicately at the left. The spirit is on his right knee, his left leg forward, his right hand raised. The servant agitatedly moves around behind them in a state of near panic.)

T'IEN SHIH: Prince, I ask you to go down on your knees and pray before the gods.

SERVANT BOY: You can't do it. You can't do it. You mustn't do it.

THE SPIRIT: The first salutation signifies proof of our union.

(They rise and face each other. The spirit bends towards her with both hands together.)

T'IEN SHIH: And with the second the waters of the Yellow River will become clear and limpid. *(She bends towards the spirit, her hands together, right foot behind left.)*

THE SPIRIT: The sacred mountain can never disappear. *(He gestures with his right hand toward the left, his left foot resting on the heel.)*

T'IEN SHIH: The Yellow River once gone leaves not a trace. *(She turns right facing front, both arms held horizontally across her body, left foot crossed in front of the right.)*

THE SPIRIT *(suddenly clutching at his stomach and making a circular*

gesture as though rubbing it, but not touching his body):
Ah . . . I feel a sharp pain in my stomach . . .

T'IEN SHIH: My prince, what is the matter? *(She goes to him, placing both hands to his left shoulder.)*

SERVANT BOY *(Gleefully runs upstage and downstage to the spirit and then to the front stage left):* Serves him right. Serves him right.

THE SPIRIT: Help me. I think I am dying. *(He waves his right hand and takes a few steps towards T'ien Shih.)* My wife . . . my servant.

SERVANT BOY: Who's your servant?

THE SPIRIT *(he bends forward several times):* Oh . . . ah.

(He exits with T'ien Shih helping him. T'ien Shih stops at the rear curtain, flings out her sleeves and sweeps round to the front. The property man places her chair and she sits with crossed hands on her knees, her sleeves falling on either side to the floor. The servant boy gestures gleefully. T'ien Shih adjusts her sleeves over her cuffs again.)

T'IEN SHIH: Oh, what bitterness. My lover is ill. *(She places her right hand to her eyes and weeps.)*

How can I express the pain in my heart? *(Her hand waves to her heart.)*

Husband, go and lie down in the study. I'll call the boy and tell him. Come here boy, come here, boy. *(She points her left hand at the servant.)*

SERVANT BOY: I won't come, I won't come.

(She extends her right hand across her waist, her third finger is bent.)

T'IEN SHIH: You come here at once. *(She extends her hands to the left.)*

SERVANT BOY *(approaching):* What for?

T'IEN SHIH: Go and ask my husband's servant what kind of illness it is that affects his master in this way and find out if there is anything we can do. *(She first extends her right hand to him, then places both hands in front of her again. She turns her palms inwards towards herself and then towards the servant, her hands extended.)*

SERVANT BOY: It's no good. He's dead. *(He flings out his right arm.)*

T'IEN SHIH *(She stands placing her hands to her hips in anger):* Go and do as you're told.

(The servant boy goes to rear center stage and calls at the curtain. T'ien Shih sits again.)

SERVANT BOY: Hey, "Two hundred and fifty." What kind of illness is it your lad is suffering from?

PAPER BOY *(behind curtain):* The gentlemen?

SERVANT BOY *(facing obliquely left):* Lad's good enough for me. The mistress wants to know what kind of illness he has.

PAPER BOY *(behind curtain):* Acute heart disease.

SERVANT BOY: Aching arse disease? *(He turns to face the front stage.)*

PAPER BOY *(behind curtain):* Heart trouble.

SERVANT BOY *(laughs and walks to front stage, both fists held up before him, the right thumb raised):* It's acute heart trouble, it seems.

T'IEN SHIH *(standing and gesturing at him with right hand):* Go and ask what is the best medicine for a cure.

SERVANT BOY *(raising his right hand in a shrug):* Can't you see he's dead.

T'IEN SHIH *(raising her left hand in threat, right arm across her waist with the right hand holding the left sleeve):* Do as I say or I'll beat you.

SERVANT BOY *(facing rear curtain):* All right, all right. I'll go. Hey, "Two hundred and fifty." What's the best medicine to cure this illness?

PAPER BOY *(behind curtain):* There's only one medicine to cure it.

SERVANT BOY: What is it, "Two hundred and fifty" and where can it be found?

PAPER BOY *(behind curtain):* It must be concocted from fresh brain of a family member.

SERVANT BOY: Ah, ah. This is impossible. You require the brain of a member of the family.

(T'ien Shih gracefully brings her right hand to her temple. Her left arm is across her chest. The servant goes to right stage.)

T'IEN SHIH: Wha-at? A family member's brain?

SERVANT BOY: It's impossible.

T'IEN SHIH: Aiya. Let me see. Since my husband died what family members are left to me? *(She rotates her hands in a gesture*

*which finally brings the palms together. Then both hands are
held forward with the third finger in each case bent. She then
brings her right index finger to her temple.)*
Ah. I've got an idea. Boy, come here! *(She beckons him, her
right hand across her body, third finger bent, left hand holding
right sleeve.)*
SERVANT BOY *(backing away, shaking his hands negatively):* I'm
not your relative.
T'IEN SHIH: Come here. *(She stands and goes towards the servant
angrily, hands on hips.)*
SERVANT BOY *(from right stage fearfully holding up his right hand
and shaking it at her):* Not so fast. What do you want me for?
T'IEN SHIH: Listen, boy. *(She holds out her left hand and touches his
right shoulder, the servant backs hurriedly away.)* Since the
master died there has only been you in the house. *(She points
left with her left hand, the right hand holding the left sleeve.)*
Therefore you are related to me. *(She gestures towards herself
with both hands, then points at boy with left hand.)*
SERVANT BOY: Eh? *(He backs away.)* What? Me your relative? I'll
eat no more of your rice! And I won't wear your clothes either.
*(He hurriedly takes off his gown and throws it down. He dashes
his headdress to the ground.)* Here, take your hat back. I'm
not staying in your house. I'm off. You can find another relative. *(He mimes stepping over the threshold with forceful gestures, then strides from the stage in high dudgeon.)*
T'IEN SHIH *(gesturing with her right hand):* Now what do you think
of that? *(She brings both hands up in front of her, palms upwards, third finger bent.)* I'd scarcely opened my mouth to
speak when the boy gets in a huff and runs off. Well, what shall
I do now? *(She steps backwards and then with a circular gesture
brings the back of her right hand gently against the palm of
her left.)*
Ah. I have another idea. *(She flicks the right "water sleeve" up
and outwards and then adjusts both sleeves over her cuffs.)*
After all, my husband has scarcely been dead one week and
his brain must still be fresh. *(The left index finger and thumb
are placed against the inside of the right third finger, the remaining fingers being gently curved.)*

I could break open the coffin with an ax to get what is needed to save my lover's life. *(Her right index finger points to her head. Her left hand is across her chest. She moves sharply round in a circle, makes a hand gesture of breaking open a coffin, her fingers and thumb are extended in alignment as she forces her hand quickly downwards.)* It's a good idea. *(She backs away a few steps, moving her hands inward with a circular movement.)* But stop. I was married to this man. How could I do such a malicious thing? *(She makes a broad rounded gesture with her right "water sleeve.")* It's a thousand times impossible. *(She shakes her head with the palms of her hands held facing outwards as she backs away obliquely to the front stage.)* I could never do such a terrible deed. *(She continues in this way until she reaches the rear of the stage right.)*

THE SPIRIT *(behind curtain):* What a bitter death is mine.

(T'ien Shih turns and backs diagonally across the stage to the left front, her hands rotating with palms almost touching. She turns front, her right arm is raised and then lowered as she points in front.)

T'IEN SHIH: Aiya! I lost one husband. Must I lose a second? *(Her right hand is placed against her temple, her left arm is across her chest, the left hand holding her right sleeve. Right foot behind the left.)* I'll break open the coffin. *(She swings her sleeves then makes a gesture with her right hand of breaking open the coffin.)* And save this young prince's life.

(Both hands are in front of her close together with palms facing outwards. She then goes to the right and stops, pointing with her index finger, the third finger and thumb touching. She backs upstage, her hands making a circular gesture, palms nearly touching. She stops, brings the back of the right hand against the palm of the left, and emphasizes this sign of decision with an affirmative nod of the head. She mimes stepping over the threshold, turns and mimes the closing of double doors, first right and then left. She circles round the stage once and flicks out her right sleeve; then both her hands are brought up to the left, the left hand higher than the right as the right sleeve is flung over her left arm. She then makes a serpentine course to the exit, beginning with short steps which quicken in pace as she goes off stage with her right hand held behind her back.)

The stage is now darkened. A paper butterfly suspended on a long, thin bamboo pole is dangled and fluttered by a stage hand concealed behind the coffin and its stand. The paper boy now appears holding an open fan. He makes a lunge to catch the butterfly between his stiffly outstretched left arm and the fan in his right hand. His movements all the time are the mechanical gestures of a puppet. The butterfly is snatched from his grasp by the manipulator and there then follows a butterfly chase by the paper boy, a complex passage of choreography, which is almost impossible to describe in writing and equally impossible for a Western actor to learn without a Chinese choreographer. Briefly, the sequence of movements may be listed as follows. After his first attempt to catch the butterfly fails, the paper boy makes a sharp wheel around to the left of the stage. His fan is now closed. He takes a squatting posture and in this position quickly shuffles across the front of the stage, his face turned to the audience; he moves towards the coffin, then turns front in an upright position again. His fan is opened once more as he circles around to the front of the stage right, stretches both hands forward, raises his right leg and then his right hand as he perceives the butterfly again. He approaches the coffin obliquely with deliberately measured steps, swings his arms out, left and right, and brings his hands together as he attempts to trap the butterfly a second time. He whirls around and opens his hands only to reveal a helpless expression to the audience when he sees he has lost it again. He now goes to the right front stage, following a serpentine course, and peers to right and left; both hands hold the open fan before him. He spies the butterfly again. This time he goes towards the coffin obliquely with deliberate steps and swings his fan wildly left, right, and left again as he makes yet another vain attempt. Again he opens his hands ruefully to the audience. He closes his fan and returns to the left front stage, following a serpentine course; he turns sharp left, and with head tilted slightly forward and limbs rigid he marches stiffly off stage in a diagonal line.

This passage of choreography which has a dramatic quality all of its own is a kind of kinesthetic pun on the title of the play. This is derived from the famous story about Chuang

Chou, the Taoist philosopher of the fourth century B.C., *who, after waking from a dream in which he had become a butterfly, said: "Now I do not know whether I was then a man dreaming I was a butterfly, or whether I am now a butterfly dreaming I am a man." The butterfly sequence also emphasizes the play's mockery of men's frailties, while on a more practical level it is a very useful technical device to bridge over the pause in action occasioned by the complete change of costume which the actress must make before the final scene.)*

Scene 3: Breaking Open the Coffin

T'ien Shih now enters from the rear. She is dressed in wide black cotton trousers and scarlet tunic with a high collar as described in the section on costume. In her right hand she carries a small ax. The scene that follows is a highly expressive ballet in which not a word is spoken but everything is enacted in mime. Again this is a dance that is impossible for Westerners to interpret without benefit of a Chinese choreographer. It is full of the most subtle nuances while being charged with emotional tensity. As a dance it makes the utmost technical demands on the performer. No Chinese stage amateur could attempt it, much less any Western equivalent. It needs a highly trained actress with a complete mastery of movement. She must be able to interpret a mounting sequence of anticipation and suspense through graceful and fluid choreographic patterns which culminate in the most violent acrobatics. The following is a general outline of the physical pattern of this scene.

When T'ien Shih enters she swings the ax aloft in her right hand, punctuating this gesture with a forceful glance. She then circles towards the center of the stage and comes to a stop. Her left arm is across her chest as she poses with her right foot behind her left. She next raises her left arm as her right arm is extended downwards and her left leg is stretched to the rear across her right leg. She turns in a clockwise direction and faces right, swinging her arm holding the ax to a horizontal position. From this pose she moves diagonally to the stage front left, her hands extended in front of her, and then backs away in the same direction from which she came. Both arms are next flung upwards, then inwards with a circular sweep, as she jumps in the air and then leaps down to a squatting position, her right foot beneath her and her left foot forward, climaxing her movements with a sharp twist of her body to the right. She examines the blade of the ax and waves her hands in disapproval of the sharpness of the blade. She moves the ax up and down indicating a need to put an edge on the blade. She stands and circles around the stage with the ax held in both hands. Finally with a gesture of decision she sticks the ax through her sash at the left and goes rear stage where she is handed a small wooden tray with a cup on it.

She backs a few steps towards the front stage and turns to face the audience. She goes to center stage, puts the tray on the ground, and goes down on her knees. She takes the cup from the tray and mimes pouring water from it. Then taking the ax from her sash she holds it with the head to the left, mimes dipping it into the water, and with a rapidly increasing tempo moves the ax backwards and forwards as though honing the blade. She tests the blade, reverses the position of the ax, and goes through the process once more. Finally she tests the cutting edge with her index finger and then her thumb. She grimaces sharply as though startled by the keen quality of the blade. Next she tests the cutting power by slicing a strand of hair drawn from over her left shoulder. Satisfied, she nods her approval and throws away the strand of severed hair; all, again, is portrayed through mime. She replaces the cup on the tray, rises, replaces the ax in her sash and returns the tray to a stagehand at the rear right. She backs away in an oblique direction, smoothing a strand of hair with her right hand and then drawing it through her teeth where she clenches it in determined fashion. This action is ACTUALLY *carried out,* NOT *mimed.*

She then checks her waist as though feeling for keys and circles the front stage counterclockwise. She turns at the rear right and moves to center stage, her back to the audience. Her hands reach up as though to unlock double doors, first pushing back the right door, then the left. She expresses alarm at her boldness and turns to face the audience, both hands tremblingly crossed on her chest. She takes a step back, left arm up, then forward again with her hands over her heart. She shakes her head as though scared. She turns, looks back again, and faces front once more, shaking her right hand in a negative gesture as she backs away several steps. She returns to the invisible doors and mimes shutting them again. Her arms are crossed over her chest again as she trembles with fright; then she backs away diagonally across stage to the rear left.

The spirit is heard to cry out backstage and T'ien Shih with an air of renewed determination backs up to the front stage in a diagonal, her palms circling against each other, the strand of hair clenched in her teeth. With a kick of her left foot she circles the stage in a broad counterclockwise sweep and pulling the ax from her sash raises it high in her right hand, her left arm held across her chest. She clenches her teeth in determination, circles round to the front left and center, then kicks with a violent movement of her feet as though pushing the doors open. Going up to the coffin, she swings the ax to the left and then to the right and steps onto the chair left of the trestle on which the coffin stands. She spits on the ax and kneels on the table with her left leg. The ax is lifted high in her right hand; she poses shaking her head rapidly and slowly crossing her eyes. Suddenly she puts the ax down, places her right hand before her eyes, points to heaven, the coffin, and herself in turn and gestures with her hand as though expressing the unthinkable nature of her intention. She steps down, replaces the ax in her sash, mimes closing the doors again, and returns to the center stage where she faces front and shakes her hands to show the impossibility of her task.

She moves to the rear stage left. Again the spirit cries out in pain from backstage and again T'ien Shih backs diagonally across the stage, her hands circling rapidly with palms facing each other. Once more she raises the ax high, makes a kicking step, circles the stage, and kicks open the doors. This time, however, she goes directly to the coffin and starts prying it open at one end with the back of the ax head. The action is performed to the incessant staccato of the brass in the stage orchestra, the tempo of sound and movement reaching a frenzied pitch. She stops and circles the stage to the left of the coffin which she again begins to pry open; grasping the edge

*of her sash she uses it to aid her leverage. Then back to the
other side of the coffin and again the same movements. Then
backing a few steps, she spits on her hands, jumps on the chair
at the side of the coffin, and makes one last might swing of the
ax right and then left at the coffin. The lid of the coffin is
pushed aside (in reality whisked away by the property man)
and Chuang Tzu rises to his feet in the coffin, a somber figure
in black.*

*T'ien Shih starts back in absolute terror, gives a leap, and
turns a somersault on the stage, coming down to support herself on her left hand. Her left leg is raised and held in this position trembling, while her right hand points quaveringly towards the coffin. Her mouth is open and a look of surprised
horror is on her face.*

CHUANG TZU: Who is it?

T'IEN SHIH: I — I — I'm T'ien Shih.

*(Chuang Tzu points with his right index and middle fingers.
The switch is supported over his right arm.)*

CHUANG TZU: T'ien Shih, do you wish to call me back. *(He extends
his hand palm upwards.)* Do you wish to call me back?

*(He holds up a lighted candle. T'ien Shih raises herself on her
right knee, stands, and goes cautiously towards Chuang Tzu
who has stepped down out of his coffin. He swings out at her
with his left arm as though striking a blow. She backs away,
stunned, to the right front stage where she collapses in a sitting
position. Then crossing her legs and clasping her hands while
bringing her head to her feet, as though she were a hedgehog,
she whirls round and round like a human ball in a circle on
the floor. Chuang Tzu with a quick step paces round the re-
volving figure in a counterclockwise direction, fiercely swinging the switch as he goes and finally striding along the front
edge of the stage to a point left. Here, swinging the switch over
his right arm, he strides with legs apart, and, bending forward
while holding his beard with his left hand, he revolves his head
in a rapidly mounting tempo so that the long plume of hair
fixed to the center of his headdress is whirled round and round
in a counterclockwise direction. As T'ien Shih finishes her
gyrations she returns to her original squatting position, supported on her right hand and pointing with her left at Chuang*

Tzu who straightens up. He grimly accuses her with the index and second finger of his left hand, the switch dangling by its loop from his fourth finger.)

CHUANG TZU: Accursed T'ien Shih. You should not have done this. You should not have done this. You should not have broken open the coffin. If I had not stopped you in time you would have split open my head. T'ien Shih, what were you trying to do? *(He makes a sharp gesture with his right hand and then points towards her, his left hand placed across his beard.*
T'ien Shih stands up, her right foot behind her left. Both hands are placed close to her body on the left side, palms upwards. She is shaking with fear.)

T'IEN SHIH: I came to show fidelity to my vows.

CHUANG TZU *(his right index finger points at her and then his hand is brought against his body, palm inwards and thumb extended vertically)*: If you came to show fidelity to your vows, why did you break open my coffin?

T'IEN SHIH: Oh husband, you don't understand. After you died a soothsayer came to the house and assured me that you would return to this world within one week of death. That is why I came to break open the coffin with this ax and save your life. *(She walks to stage right front, right hand horizontally extended to the right and then left. Her left arm is across her waist, the second finger supporting the right elbow. She makes a gesture with the thumb and third finger together as she points with the index finger. Her left foot is placed behind the right as she makes a quick gesture of breaking open the coffin with her right hand. She runs towards him but he brushes her angrily away.)*

CHUANG TZU: Look at your embroidered clothes. They hardly seem suitable for a faithful widow. *(He gestures contemptuously at her.)*

T'IEN SHIH *(her hands placed across her chest, then dropped)*: What? Oh, these clothes. *(She faces front, right hand to her temple, left arm across her waist.)*
Husband, don't you understand that it was a great joy for me to break open the coffin. An occasion for celebration and not for mourning. *(She extends both arms down her body.)*

CHUANG TZU *(curtly)*: No doubt. Bring me some tea. *(He places the*

*end of the switch on the back of his left hand, holding it ver-
tically with his right hand.)*

T'IEN SHIH: All right. Ah, father in heaven, how did you restore
him to life? *(She backs away from Chuang Tzu. Bending to
pick up the ax and trying to conceal it under her right arm,
she goes to center stage and dropping the ax by mistake, steps
back in alarm.)*

CHUANG TZU: T'ien Shih, I want to ask you a question. Are there
any men in the world more divine than Chuang Tzu? *(He
points at her with thumb and second finger together.)*

T'IEN SHIH: Many many more than you. *(Chuang Tzu spits at her.)*

CHUANG TZU: Where are these many, many more? Obviously there
is the Prince of Ch'u-kuo. When he came to express his condolences you found him superior to all men and extremely
handsome and asked him to stay here so that you could marry him. Afterwards when he was suddenly taken ill, you broke
open my coffin with your ax to get my brain for the cure to
save his life. Isn't that so? *(He raises his right hand high above
his forehead, thumb vertical, then brings his hands, palms
down, making a sharp movement of disdain with his right
hand which then circles against his beard. Finally he slaps
both hands together and extends them in query.)*

T'IEN SHIH *(defiantly):* To catch the thief —

CHUANG TZU: One needs the stolen goods. *(He points at her.)*

T'IEN SHIH: To seize adulterers — *(She circles both hands upwards
then down to a pointing gesture, second finger and thumb
together, index finger extended, both hands.)*

CHUANG TZU: One needs the pair.

*(T'ien Shih raises her right hand to her temple, left arm
across her chest, left second finger under her right elbow.
Then she gestures with both hands towards Chuang Tzu,
back of her right hand in the palm of her left; finally she
places both hands on her hips.)*

T'IEN SHIH: A Buddhist priest's cap on a Taoist's head. Show me
the proof.

CHUANG TZU *(shaking his extended right hand with the palm downwards):* I warn you, you won't like it.

T'IEN SHIH: I still want to see your proof. *(She faces him, hands on
hips. She puts both hands to his right arm and he pushes her*

violently away. She swings away in a circle with her right hand raised and left arm across her waist.)

CHUANG TZU: Wait a minute.

(He raises his arm and the spirit rushes in from the rear left and goes to embrace T'ien Shih. Chuang Tzu separates them with a wave of the switch and backs away a few paces with left hand raised. The spirit raises his right sleeve, turns, and with long swift steps exits at the rear left. Chuang Tzu goes to left front stage, then to center stage, his hand to his beard.)

T'IEN SHIH: Oh, heaven above. This is the end.

(She steps forward and goes down on her knees and raises both hands above her with the index fingers together. Next she picks up the ax in her right hand and stands swinging round. She puts the ax to her left shoulder and poses, right foot behind the left. Her left hand is across her waist. She bends back and mimes cutting her throat with the ax, her eyes crossing in an agonized expression before she falls diagonally to the right and then runs off quickly. Chuang Tzu laughs sardonically.)

CHUANG TZU: It is done! Ho, ho, ho.

(He strides majestically and deliberately from the stage, flicking his switch as he goes.)

THE END

Appendix   Glossary   Index

Appendix

Excerpts from *Ssu Lang Visits His Mother*

The two plays translated here both use music based on the *hsi-p'i* mode previously mentioned. The various passages recorded constitute excerpts of music and dialogue which will provide the reader with aural illustration of some forms discussed earlier in the description of theater music (see pp. 6–9).

First Excerpt

This illustrates the combination of spoken word, song, and tone rhythm which is so typical of Chinese stage practice, and at the same time it is a good example of conventions which are frequently used in formal sequence to open the play. After the preliminary entry of the actor playing Ssu Lang, which the reader will find described in detail on page 33, he recites the *yin-tzu* which consists of the following three lines, half-recited, half-sung, and finally treated as pure sound effect by elongating the rhythm of the syllables:

> Chin chin so wu-t'ung
> Ch'ang t'an sheng sui,
> I chen na feng.

Literally this could be translated as "the *wu-t'ung* tree locked in a golden courtyard, a long sigh carried away on the breeze." It constitutes a poetic reference to Ssu Lang's own captivity. The first line, *chin chin so wu-t'ung*, is recited in the stylized speech of the *sheng* actor, but the second and third lines are half sung, the last two words in the second line, *sheng sui*, being prolonged while the second word *chen* in the third line is held through the space of several syllables rising and falling in rhythmic sequence.

After the *yin-tzu* the actor walks to the chair placed center stage as described on page 34, and seating himself he performs *tso ch'ang shih*, literally, "doing the stage poem." This consists of four lines with identical rhyme endings rendered in the heightened speech characteristic of the role. They are:

> Shih lo fan pang shih wu nien
> Yen kuo heng yang ko i t'ien
> Kao t'ang lao mu nan te chien
> Tsen pu chiao jen lui lien lien

With these poetic lines Ssu Lang establishes his situation, i.e., after being exiled in a barbarian state for fifteen years the seasons have passed, and he has never been able to see his mother, and so he weeps.

Following this passage he then performs *t'ung ming*, "name recital": *Pen kung Ssu Lang Yen-hui*; literally, "this person is Ssu Lang Yen-hui." After this he goes on to name both his parents, to tell how their family was decimated in battle and how he himself came to be in his present circumstances.

YIN-TZU

Ssu Lang:
> Chin chin so wu-t'ung
> Ch'ang . . . . t'an sheng sui
> I chen . . . . na . . . . feng . . . .

TSO CH'ANG SHIH

> *(Note the rhyming endings of the four lines.)*
> Shih lo fan pang shih wu nien
> Yen kuo heng yang ko i t'ien
> Kao t'ang lao mu nan te chien
> Tsen pu chiao jen lui lien lien

T'UNG MING

Pen kung Ssu Lang Yen-hui
Wo fu Chin-tao ling kung
Wo mu She-shih t'ai-chün
Chih yin shih wu nien ch'ien
Sha-t'an fu hui
Na i ch'ang hsüeh chan
Chih sha te wo Yang chia ssu tsou t'ao wang
Pen kung pei ch'in
To meng t'ai-hou pu chan
Fan chiang kung-chu p'i p'ei
Tso jih hsiao fan pao tao
Hsiao T'ien-tso tsai chiu lung fei hu yü
Pai hsia t'ien men ta chen
Sung wang yü chia ch'in cheng
Wo mu chieh ya liang ts'ao
Yeh lai tao pei fan
Wo yu hsin ch'ü tao Sung ying
Chien mu i mien
Tsen nai kuan chin tsu ke
Ch'a chih yeh nan i fei kuo
Ssu hsiang ch'i lai
Hao pu shang kan
Ai — jen yeh.

Second Excerpt

The audience is now prepared for a lengthy sung passage whose spirited rhythms and poetic lines emphasize the plight of the hero within the imaginations of the onlookers. This is the second excerpt on the tape. It is called "Sitting in the Palace," *Tso Kung*, in reference to the first line and opens in *hsi-p'i man-pan* timing, i.e., a rhythm of one accented and three unaccented beats.

This song is one of the well-loved pieces in the play. It was the kind of air that in the old theater set heads nodding and hands silently beating out the rhythms as the audience surrendered themselves to it. Peking theater airs were concise and limited but their emotional impact was immediate on the audience. Every line and stanza was an entity. The musical style was intended to be neither too complex nor too deep by Chinese standards but simple enough to convey mood and atmosphere in the most direct way within the technical possibilities.

In this song, when the hero is sitting in the palace sighing for the days behind him, he emphasizes his state of captivity by means of several poetic references whose syllabic contents are chosen with a view to the sound pattern required and consistent with the rhyming scheme used in the Peking theater. There are certain key rhythms such as the slow beat, *man-pan*; the quick beat, *k'uai-pan*; the swaying beat, *yao-pan*; and so on. A feature of Chinese theatrical singing is the way the performer suddenly changes over from one rhythm to another to intensify atmosphere or change the mood in the middle of a song passage. In "Sitting in the Palace" the actor first sings in the slow beat which is used to suggest a man in a reflective or melancholy state of mind. When he gets to the point where he describes the bloody battle which led to his capture he changes rhythm, this time to the so-called two-six beat, *erh-liu*, which suggests heightened tension in keeping with the subject matter. Finally toward the end of his song when he is bewailing his separation from his mother in these words, "if I wish to meet my mother it can only be in a dream," the singer changes to the swaying beat, yao-pan, suggesting mental agitation and restlessness.

Throughout this song the functions of the various orchestral instruments are well marked. The stringed *hu-ch'in*, the principal accompanying instrument, has an intensely supple quality well suited to the rhythmic juxtapositions involved whereas the drum, castanets, and gong beat out the pace and emphasize climaxes. As an undertone to this the moon-guitar and the *san-hsien* provide a continuous flow within the melodic pattern. The "through the door," *kuo-men*, passages mentioned in the section on music are also clearly heard as the connecting passages between lines. Above all, it is possible to distinguish clearly the way that each word is treated purely as a unit of tonal pattern within the context of the song.

CH'ANG HSI-P'I MAN-PAN

Yang Yen ....[1] hui .... tso kung yuan .... (*hsiao kuo-men*)

1. The dots in the excerpts of singing indicate the exact number of beats on which the preceding word is drawn out.

Tzu .... ssu .... tzu t'an .... (*ta kuo-men*)

Hsiang ch'i liao .... tang nien shih (*hsiao kuo-men*)

Hao .... pu .... tsan .... jan .... (*ta kuo-men*)

Wo hao pi .... lung .... chung niao .... (*hsiao kuo-men*)

Yu .... ch'ih .... nan .... chan .... (*ta kuo-men*)

Wo hao pi .... hu li shan (*hsiao kuo-men*)

Shou .... liao .... ku .... tan (*ta kuo-men*)

Wo hao pi ..... nan lai yen ....

.... (*hsiao kuo-men*)

shih ch'ün .... fei .... san ....

.... (*ta kuo-men*)

Wo hao pi .... ch'ien shui lung (*hsiao kuo-men*)

k'un .... tsai .... sha-t'an ....

Hsiang tang nien .... Sha-t'an .... hui ......

(*hsiao kuo-men*)

chuan erh-liu.

I ch'ang hsüeh .... chan .... chih .... sha te ....

.... hsüeh .... ch'eng ho shih ku ....

tui .... shan ....

Chih .... sha .... te ....

Yang chia .... chiang tung t'ao .... hsi ....

san ......

Chih .... sha .... te ....

Chung erh lang kun .... hsia .... ma an ....

Wo .... pei .... ch'in ....

kai .... ming .... hsing fang t'o .... tz'u .....

nan ......

chiang .... Yang tzu .... ch'e .....

mu i

p'i p'ei .... liang yüan ....

Hsiao .... T'ien-tso .... pai .... t'ien men liang hsia

.... hui chan .... wo .... ti ni-

ang ....

ya .... liang ts'ao lai .... pei fan ....
....
Wo .... yu .... hsin .... hui .... Sung ying
chien mu ....
i .... mien ....
Tsen .... nai wo .... shen tsai fan
yüan .... ko
tsai t'ien .... pien .... szu .... lao .... mu
....
pu yu erh kan ch'ang .... t'ung .... tuan
.... hsiang .... lao niang ....
chung jih li
chu lei .... pu kan yen .... cheng cheng.
Kao t'ang mu
nan te
chien
erh ti lao niang
yao hsiang feng chu fei shih meng
li t'uan yüan

Third Excerpt

In the third musical excerpt we have the first entry of the Princess. Her voice is heard calling to her maid before she breaks into a song whose rhythm is known in Chinese as "flowing water beat," *liu-shui pan*. Its light, free, and indeed flowing quality here suggests a feminine mood as the Princess sings: "The peonies are in flower, masses of red blossom. How glorious the spring with the birds all singing." The characteristic high-pitched vocal quality of the female role with its sustained falsetto and almost birdlike character is clearly demonstrated here. It is entirely artificial and makes no pretense at any natural quality. It is a method of vocal symbolism devised for a theater that formerly used only actors to play women's roles. Before the entry of the Princess her advent is announced by the beating of the small gong in the orchestra, always the signal for the entry of a female character. After the song there follows one or two lines of dialogue taken from the text to illustrate the quality of the speaking voice in both the male and female roles.

KUNG CHU: Ya-t'ou
YA T'OU: Yu.
KUNG CHU: Tai lu-a.
YA T'OU: Shih-la.
KUNG CHU *(ch'ang liu-shui-pan):*
  Shao yao k'ai mou-tan fang hua hung i pien yen yang t'ien ch'ün kuang
  Hao pai niao sheng wo pen tang yü fu-ma hsiao ch'ien yu wan
SSU LANG *(pai):* K'o niang ah
KUNG CHU *(pai):* Ya!
  Tsen nai t'a chung jih li ch'ou so mei chien
  Fu-ma tsa chia lai liao
SSU LANG *(pai):* Kung-chu lai liao ch'ing tso.
KUNG CHU *(pai):* Fu-ma ch'ing tso.
YA T'OU *(pai):* Ch'ing fu-ma yeh ti an
SSU LANG *(pai):* Pu hsiao. K'o.

Fourth Excerpt

The fourth passage is a good example of a Peking stage duet. The Princess and her husband sing in quick beat rhythm whose feeling is well conveyed here. An attitude of mounting expectation is created. The rhythm-marking function of the castanets and the background confirmation of this by the string instruments is well conveyed in this passage which begins:

  We have been a happy couple, dear wife.
  Worthy Princess, do not be so modest.
  If one day my furrowed brow loses its frown
  I shall not forget your favors weighty as mountains.
The Princess sings:
  Husband, what are you saying?
  Although you and I in North and South
  Were separated by a thousand li
  We married.

Why do you sit all day with furrowed brow?
If you have a secret, please tell it me.

Her husband goes on to explain how a battle has been planned by the Chinese armies with his mother in charge of supplies and how he longs to visit the camp to see his mother. The Princess counters with:

Why let words put you off?
If you wish to visit your mother I shall not hinder you.
Her husband replies:
Princess, although you will not interfere
It is in vain without the arrow of command.
She sings:
I fear in my heart that if I give you the arrow
You will go and never return.
He replies:
Princess, if you give me the arrow
I will return at the fifth watch before dawn breaks.
The Princess expresses doubt in these words:
The Sung camp is far from here.
How can you return in one night?
He answers:
Princess, with the whip applied to a swift horse
I can return in one night.

SSU LANG *(ch'ang k'uai-pan):*
Kung-chu
Wo ho ni hao fu-ch'i en te pu ch'ien
Hsien Kung-chu yu ho pi li i t'ai ch'ien
Yang Yen-hui yu i jih ch'ou mei te chan
Shih pu wang hsien kung-chu en chung ju shan.
KUNG CHU *(chieh ch'ang):*
Fu-ch'i men chiang shen-ma en te pu ch'ien
Tsa yü ni ko nan pei ch'ien li yin yüan
Yin ho ku tsung jih li ch'ou mei pu chan
Yu shen-ma hsin fu shih ni chih kuan ming yen
SSU LANG *(chieh ch'ang):*
Fei shih wo che chi jih ch'ou mei pu chan
Yu i chien hsin fu shih pu kan ming yen

Hsiao T'ien-tso pai t'ien-men liang kuo chiao chan
Wo ti niang ya liang ts'ao lai tao pei fan
Wo yu hsin tao Sung ying chien mu-i mien
Tsen nai wo shen tsai fan nan i ch'ü kuan.

KUNG CHU *(chieh ch'ang k'uai-pan):*
Ni na li hsiu te yao ch'iao yen lai pien
Ni yao t'an kao t'ang mu tsa pu tsu lan

SSU LANG *(chieh ch'ang k'uai-pan):*
Kung-chu tsung k'en hsing fang
Keng wu yu ling-chien yeh wang jan

KUNG CHU *(chieh ch'ang k'uai-pan):*
Yu hsin tseng ni ti chin p'i chien
P'a ni i ch'ü chiu pu hui huan

SSU LANG *(chieh ch'ang k'uai-pan):*
Kung-chu tseng wo chin p'i chien
Wu ku t'ien-ming chi k'o huan

KUNG CHU *(ch'ang k'uai-pan):*
Sung ying li tz'u lu t'u yuan i yeh
Chih chien ni tsen neng kou huan

SSU LANG *(ch'ang k'uai-pan):*
Chih Kuan fang ta tan k'uai ma ju pien i yeh huan

Fifth Excerpt

In the last excerpt we hear the two clowns, court officials who are nicknamed "National Uncles" in the play. They keep up a rapid fire of cross talk, the clowns being the only characters on the traditional stage who are allowed to use the Peking colloquial and to improvise in it. In this scene they are advising the Princess to gain her mother's sympathy by pretending to commit suicide and abandon her child. When the Princess demurs they sing out in an alternating chorus:

You are very foolish, if you give up the little one . . .
. . . then you save the big one . . .
. . . if you don't want to give up the little one . . .
. . . then how can you save the big one . . .
. . . if you save the big one . . .
. . . in the future there will be lots of new little ones.

The Princess replies:
Oh, stop talking rubbish but let me try.

ERH KUO CHIU *(pai):*
Wo shuo Kung-chu che shih shen-ma
Shih hou la ni hai shih i ko ching erh ti yao ch'iao ch'iang
K'uai na chu-i pa
KUNG CHU *(pai):*
Shih tao ho chin wo shih i tien chu-i yeh mi yu la
Erh wei kuo-chiu yu shen ma kao chien ma
ERH KUO CHIU *(pai):*
Wo lai wen wen ni tang chu tao ling ti shih-hou
Shih ta ts'ung shui shen shang so ch'i ah
KUNG CHU *(pai):*
Tang chu tao ling ti shih hou
Shi ta A Ko shen shang so ch'i ah
ERH KUO CHIU *(pai):*
Na ma ni hai shih ta A Ko
Shen shang lai ah.
KUNG CHU *(pai):*
Yu
Wo ta A Ko shen shang
Tsen ma lai ah
EHR KUO CHIU *(t'ung pai):*
Wo lai kao su ni, ni pa A Ko wang lao T'ai Hou shen shang
che ma i chih
Na pao-ch'ien chia chuang mo po tzu hsun ssu
T'ai-hou i hsin t'ung wai sun tzu
Che ko jen ch'ing k'o chiu chun la
KUNG CHU *(pai):*
Oh. Pa A Ko wang wo mu-hou shen shang i jung
Wo na pao-chien chia chuang mo po tzu hsun ssu ah
EHR KUO CHIU *(t'ung):*
Tui la k'o shih chia-ti pieh
chen wang po tzu shang tsa
KUNG CHU *(pai):*
Pu ch'eng pu ch'eng
EHR KUO CHIU *(pai):*
Tsen ma pu ch'eng

KUNG CHU *(pai):*
    Yao shih hsia che A Ko
    Na ko tsen-ma hao ah
    Wo k'e shih pu te wo-ti erh-tzu
KUO CHIU CHIA *(pai):*
    Ni ch'ao ni to sha
    Ni yao shih she liao hsiao-ti
KUO CHIU I *(pai):*
    Chiu chiu liao-ti
KUO CHIU CHIA *(pai):*
    Ni yao shih she pu liao hsiao-ti
KUO CHIU I *(pai):*
    Na k'e chiu chiu pu liao lao-ti
KUO CHIU CHIA *(pai):*
    Ni yao shih chiu liao lao-ti
KUO CHIU I *(pai):*
    Chiang lai yao to shao hsiao-ti mei yu ah
KUNG CHU *(pai):*
    Ai pieh hu shuo pa tao la
    Tai wo lai shih shih

Glossary

Translator's Note

The Wade system of romanization, used throughout this text, is tiresome and confusing to those who have not studied it, and no practical purpose would be served by reproducing its rules and regulations here. The following elementary points may be useful to remember when reading the terms mentioned in this text:

ao makes an approximate English sound of *ow*.
ch is pronounced roughly like *j*, e.g., *cheng*: jeng.
ch' aspirates approximately as it looks, e.g., *ch'eng*: cheng, the *e* in this word being nearer to *u* in run than *e* in hen.
k is hard like the English *g*, e.g., *kan*: gan, *kuo*: gwor.
k' aspirated is approximately as it looks, e.g., *k'uai-pan*: kwai ban.
p is hard like the English *b*, e.g., *pan*: ban.
t is hard like the English *d*, e.g., *tan*: dan.
t' aspirated is approximately as it looks, e.g., *t'i*: tee.
j is roughly like the English *r*, e.g., *jan*: ran.

Romanized Terms Used in the Text

an erh-i: stage costume used for a child character.
ao: stage costume worn by women characters; a waist length tunic with a high collar and having long sleeves but no water sleeves.

cheng-kuan: gesture used by actors; the temples are lightly touched with the fingers of both hands as though adjusting headdress.
cheng-pu: the normal pace or step for the sheng actor.
cheng-tan: a classification of the women's roles.

160

ch'i-hsüeh: special shoes which have small stilts built into the center of the soles, worn by the actress playing in Manchu style costume.

ch'i-mang: stage robe worn by an actress and based on Manchu ceremonial costume.

ch'i-p'ao: robe worn by actresses and based on the ordinary dress of Manchu women used earlier in the century; the prototype of the modern Chinese woman's gown.

ching: the painted-face role on the Peking stage, played by actors only.

ching-hsi: Peking drama; literally, "drama of the capital."

ch'ing-i: a woman's role played by actors as well as actresses in the past and characterized by accomplished singing.

ch'ou: the comic roles on the Peking stage.

ch'ü: a generic term for a song poem.

ch'ün-tzu: skirt worn in the women's roles.

erh-hu: stringed instrument used in the stage orchestra.

erh-huang: one of the two principal musical modes used on the Peking stage.

erh-liu: musical timing; literally, two-six rhythm of one accented and one unaccented beat.

fan-hsiu: a sleeve movement; literally, "turned sleeve."

fu-ma t'ao-ch'ih: headdress worn only by Ssu Lang and symbolizing a Chinese of high rank living as a barbarian of equally high status.

fu-tzu: hair switch carried by Buddhist priests; the prototype for an identical article used as a stage property and called *ying-ch'en* in the greenroom.

hsi-p'i: one of the two principal musical modes used on the Peking stage.

hsi-p'i man-pan: slow timing used in the above.

hsi-p'i tao-pan: tao-pan, timing with no set numerical beat in the hsi-p'i mode.

hsiao-i: stage costume worn by a servant boy in mourning.

hsiao kuo-men: literally, "small through the door"; a passage played on the *hu-ch'in* (q.v.) in the stage orchestra and serving as a connective between the actor's songs.

hsiao-lo: the small gong in the stage orchestra.

hsiao-lo ta-shang: passage played on the gongs in the stage orchestra to indicate a person of dignity is in his home or place of office.

hsiao-sheng: a classification of the male role; the young hero.

hsiu-hua ch'ün tzu: long wrap over skirt worn by actresses (or female impersonators), having a rectangular embroidered panel down the front.

hua-tan: a classification of the womens' roles on the Peking stage; the coquette or maidservant.

hua ying hsieh-tzu: ornamental robe worn by the *hsiao-sheng* actor.

hu-ch'in: two stringed instrument played with an attached bow; the principal accompanying instrument to the actor's singing on the Peking stage.

hung ying-mao: stage headdress; a hat worn in the comic roles and based on the old Manchu official style.

jung-ch'iu: silk floss pompon worn as a decoration in different styles of stage headdress.

kao fang-chin: stage headdress; the hat of a scholar.

k'u-tzu: silk or cotton trousers.

k'uai-pan: musical term meaning quick time.

kuan-hsüeh: black satin boots with high soles worn by male characters on the Peking stage.

k'un-ch'ü: lyrical dramatic form which preceded the Peking style drama and originated in the K'unshan district of central China.

kung-tiao: a musical term translatable as mode.

kuo-men: literally, "through the door"; connective passages played on the *hu-ch'in* during the actor's singing

lao-sheng: the bearded male roles.

lao-tan: the aged women parts always played by actors in the past.

liang pa t'ou-erh: stage headdress worn in women's roles and based on the style formerly worn by Manchu ladies of high standing.

li jan-k'ou: stage gesture; stroking the beard from top to bottom with the right hand.

liu-shui-pan: literally, "flowing water beat"; a musical term used to signify a light and free rhythm.

lung-t'ao: stage supernumeraries who represent armies, court retainers, and so on.

lung-t'ou kuai-chang: a long wooden staff with an ornamental dragon's head carved at the top; it is always carried by the *lao-tan* actors.

ma-pien: the silk tasseled switch used to symbolize riding a horse on the Chinese stage.

ma-t'i hsiu: literally, "horse hoof sleeves"; sleeves with turned up cuffs used on certain stage costumes worn in the male roles.

man-jan: the full beard worn in leading male roles and made of horsehair.

man-pan: a musical term meaning slow timing.

mang: official robe worn in both male and female roles.

nü hsiao-i: stage costume worn by female characters in mourning.

nü kuan-i: three quarter length robe worn by *lao-tan* actor.

pan: a musical term, the accented beat within the measure; also an orchestral instrument, clappers or time-beater used by the orchestra leader.

pang-tzu: a local dramatic form which influenced the development of the Peking style.

p'ao-t'ao: robe worn by comic actors and based on the old Manchu official gown.

pei-hsin: stage costume worn in the womens' roles; an outdoor garment. It has no sleeves, opens down the front, and has slits at either side; the materials used are silk or satin often highly embroidered.

p'i: generic term for a stage costume having no sleeves or collar and worn three-quarter length; an outdoor garment.

pu ao: stage costume worn in *hua-tan* roles; a waist length tunic with a high collar, exactly the same style as the *ao* (q.v.) but made of cotton.

san-hsien: three stringed instrument played with a plectrum and used as secondary accompaniment on the Peking stage; it is the prototype of the Japanese samisen.

san-man pan: literally, broken slow beat.

san-pan: literally, scattered or broken beat.

sheng: male roles.

shih-shih hsüeh-tzu: stage costume worn in women's roles. It is knee length, opens down the front, has a high collar and "water sleeves"; it is made of silk.

shuai-fa: a horsehair plume worn on the crown of the head and symbolizing a hero in distress or captivity.

so-na: a reed instrument used in the stage orchestra for special indications.

ta feng kua: headdress worn by an Empress and based on ceremonial Manchu style.

ta kuo-men: literally, "big through the gate"; long connective passages played on the *hu-ch'in* (q.v.) during the stage action and singing.

ta-lo ch'ung-t'ou: passage on large gong to indicate actor's entry.

ta-t'ou: the standard hair style worn in the women's roles on the Peking stage. It is said to have been devised by Wei Ch'ang-sheng, an actor who went to Peking from Szechuan about 1779.

tan: women's roles.

tan-p'i ku: the small hardwood drum on a tripod used by the orchestra leader on the Peking stage.

tao-pan: a rhythm with no fixed numerical beat.

ti-tzu: seven-holed bamboo flute.

tou-hsiu: sleeve movement used as a decorative signal or terminating point during the actor's performance.

wu-sheng: male roles characterized by fighting and acrobatic techniques.

wu-tan: female role characterized by fighting and acrobatic techniques.

yang and *yin*: traditional symbol of creation in ancient China and a talisman against misfortune; used as a motif on the *pa-kua i*, a robe worn by characters with special magic powers.

yao-pan: musical term, literally "swaying beat"; a rhythm suggesting mental agitation.

yin-tzu: two or four lines, half-sung half-recited, used as standard entry procedure by the actor.

ying-ch'en. See *fu-tzu*.

yü-tai: the stiff hooplike girdle always worn with the *mang* (q.v.) robe.

yuan-pan: musical timing, moderate.

yueh-ch'in: a musical instrument having four strings plucked with a plectrum and a circular sound box which has given it the name "moon guitar"; it is used for secondary accompaniment on the Peking stage.

Index